BART SIMPSON
TO THE RESCUE!

TITAN BOOKS

BART SIMPSON TO THE RESCUE!

Collects Bart Simpson *53-54 and 56-58*

Published in the UK by Titan Books, a division of Titan Publishing Group Ltd.,
144 Southwark St., London SE1 0UP, under licence from Bongo Entertainment, Inc.

FIRST EDITION: JANUARY 2014

ISBN 9781783290710

2 4 6 8 10 9 7 5 3 1

Publisher: Matt Groening
Creative Director: Nathan Kane
Managing Editor: Terry Delegeane
Director of Operations: Robert Zaugh
Art Director: Chia-Hsien Jason Ho
Art Director Special Projects: Serban Cristescu
Assistant Art Director: Mike Rote
Production Manager: Christopher Ungar
Assistant Editor: Karen Bates
Production: Nathan Hamill, Art Villanueva
Administration: Ruth Waytz, Pete Benson
Editorial Assistant: Max Davison
Legal Guardian: Susan A. Grode

Printed by TC Transcontinental, Beauceville, QC, Canada. 02/05/14

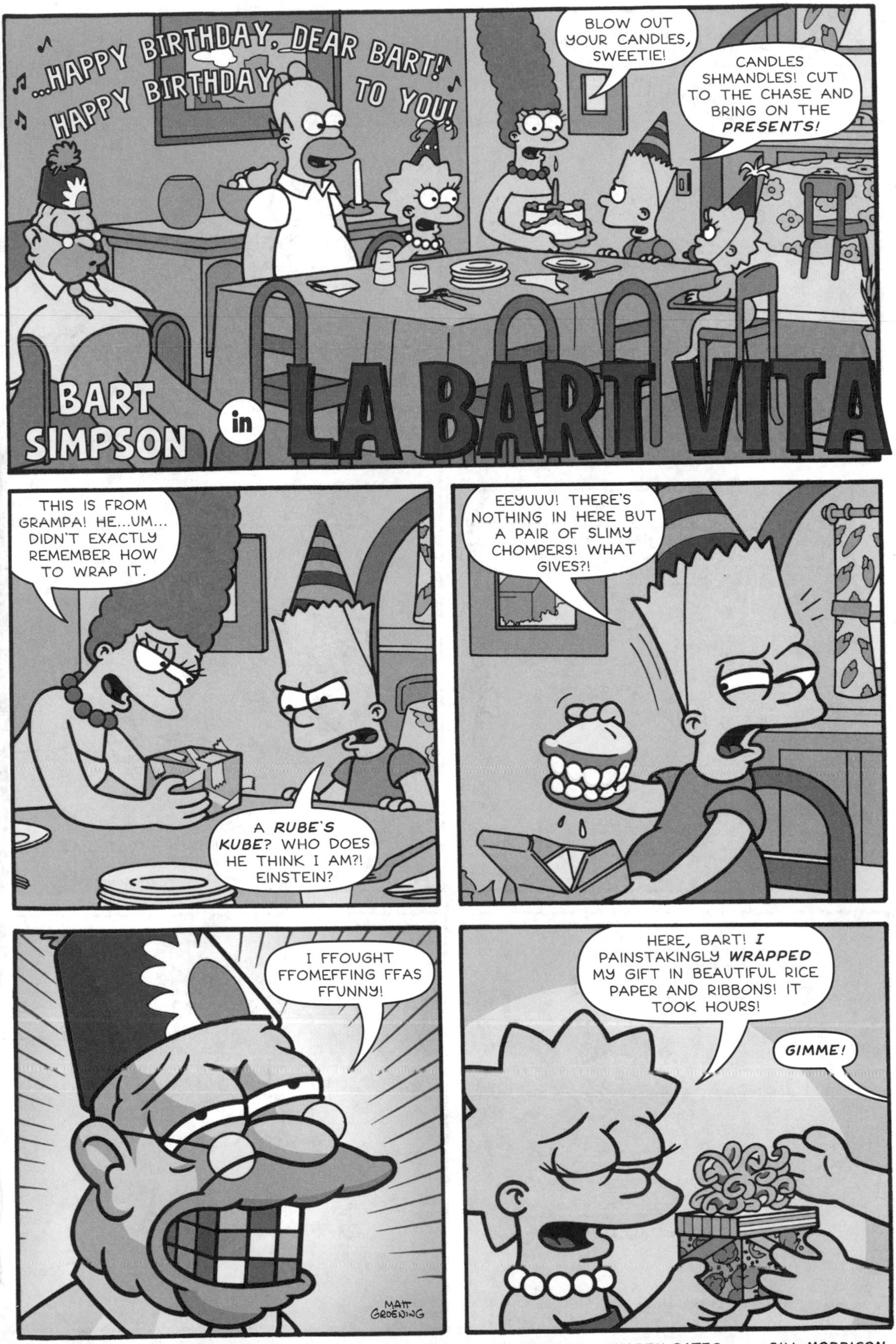
...HAPPY BIRTHDAY, DEAR BART! HAPPY BIRTHDAY TO YOU!
BLOW OUT YOUR CANDLES, SWEETIE!
CANDLES SHMANDLES! CUT TO THE CHASE AND BRING ON THE PRESENTS!
BART SIMPSON
in
LA BART VITA
THIS IS FROM GRAMPA! HE...UM... DIDN'T EXACTLY REMEMBER HOW TO WRAP IT.
A RUBE'S KUBE? WHO DOES HE THINK I AM?! EINSTEIN?
EEYUUU! THERE'S NOTHING IN HERE BUT A PAIR OF SLIMY CHOMPERS! WHAT GIVES?!
I FFOUGHT FFOMEFFING FFAS FFUNNY!
MATT GROENING
HERE, BART! I PAINSTAKINGLY WRAPPED MY GIFT IN BEAUTIFUL RICE PAPER AND RIBBONS! IT TOOK HOURS!
GIMME!

PAT MCGREAL SCRIPT · *JOHN COSTANZA* PENCILS · *PHYLLIS NOVIN* INKS · *ALAN HELLARD* COLORS · *KAREN BATES* LETTERS · *BILL MORRISON* EDITOR

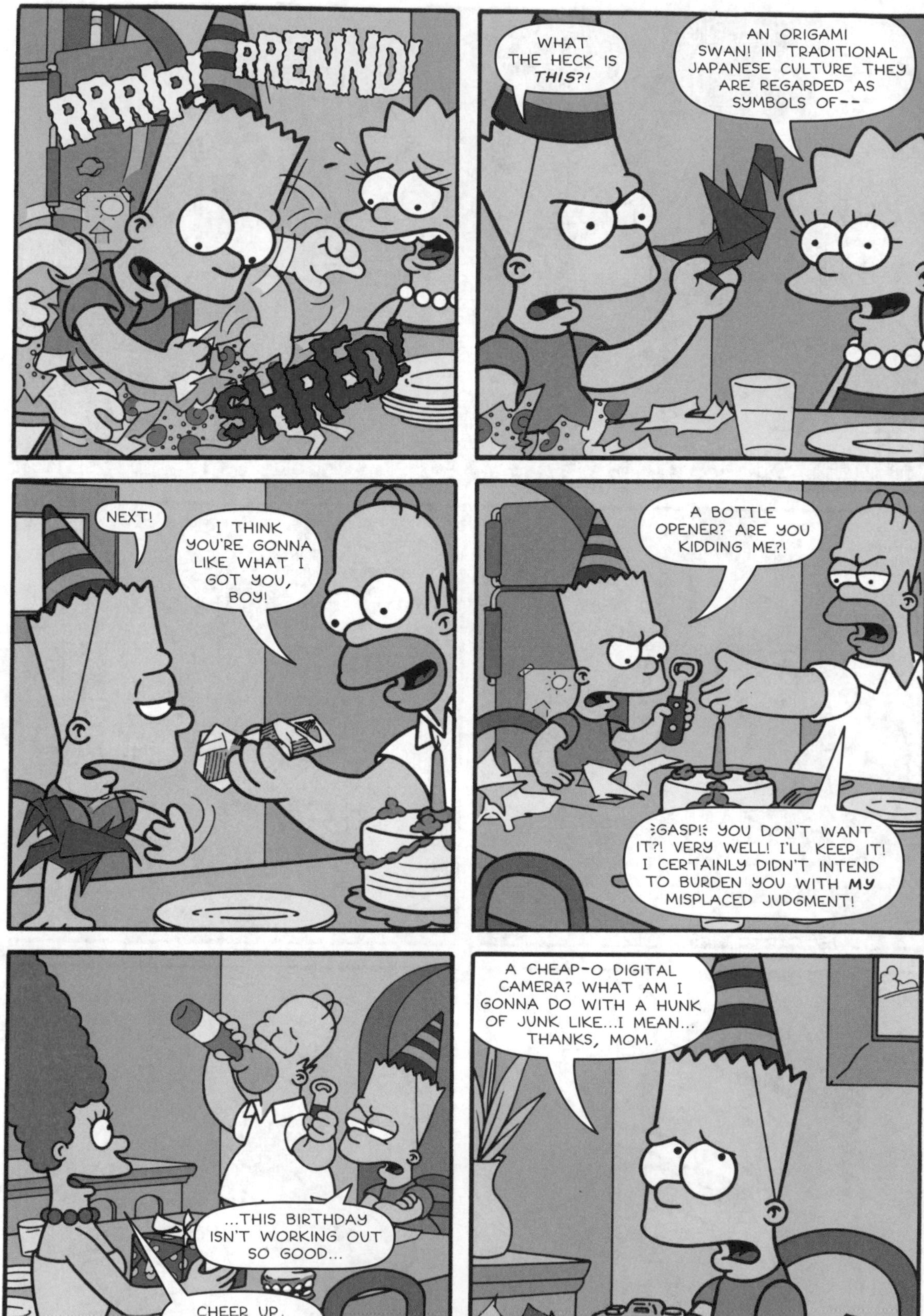
RRRIP!
RRENND!
SHRED!
WHAT THE HECK IS THIS?!
AN ORIGAMI SWAN! IN TRADITIONAL JAPANESE CULTURE THEY ARE REGARDED AS SYMBOLS OF--
NEXT!
I THINK YOU'RE GONNA LIKE WHAT I GOT YOU, BOY!
A BOTTLE OPENER? ARE YOU KIDDING ME?!
:GASP!: YOU DON'T WANT IT?! VERY WELL! I'LL KEEP IT! I CERTAINLY DIDN'T INTEND TO BURDEN YOU WITH MY MISPLACED JUDGMENT!
...THIS BIRTHDAY ISN'T WORKING OUT SO GOOD...
CHEER UP, SWEETIE! HERE'S MY PRESENT!
A CHEAP-O DIGITAL CAMERA? WHAT AM I GONNA DO WITH A HUNK OF JUNK LIKE...I MEAN... THANKS, MOM.

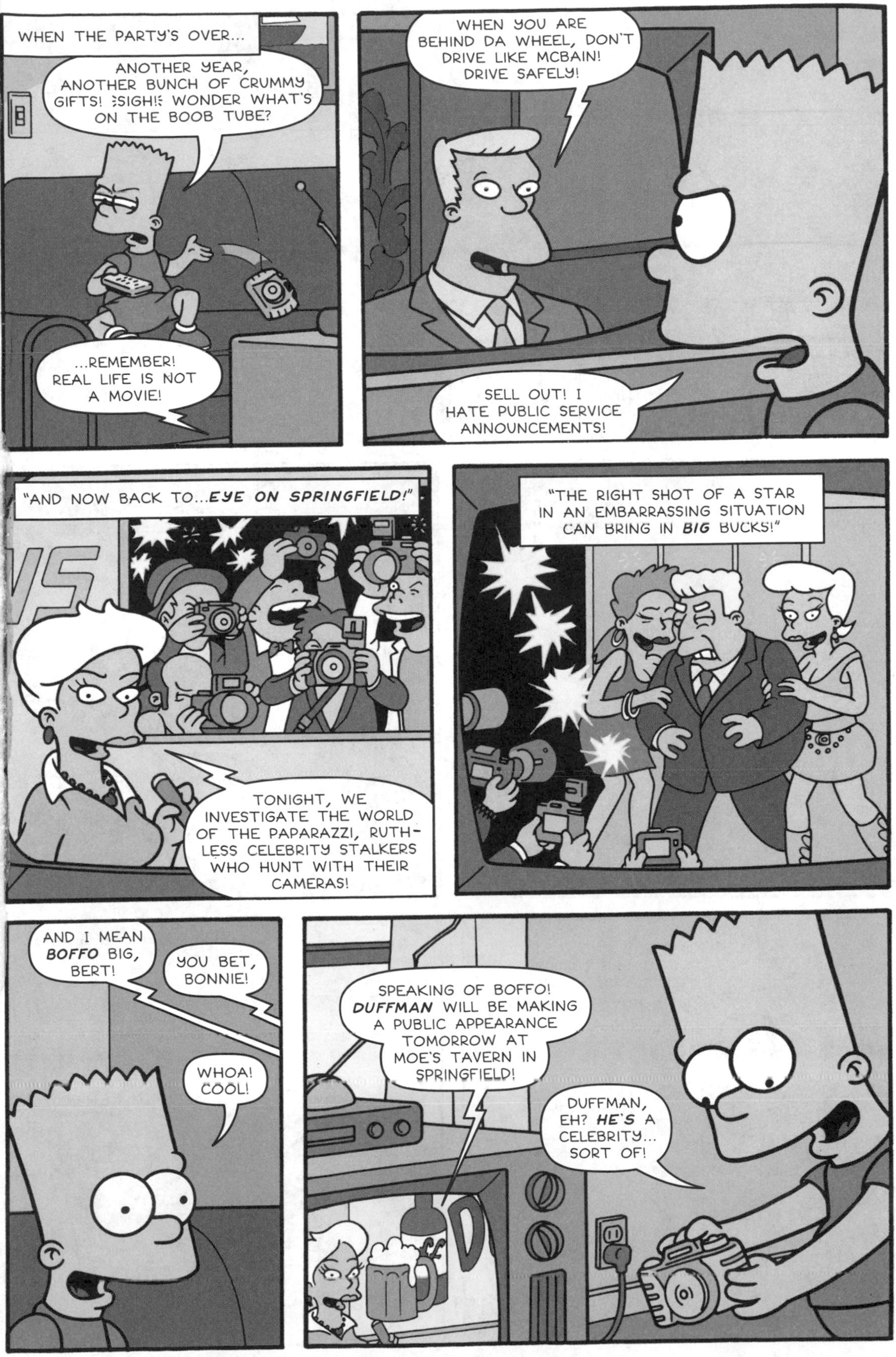

WHEN THE PARTY'S OVER...
ANOTHER YEAR, ANOTHER BUNCH OF CRUMMY GIFTS! :SIGH!: WONDER WHAT'S ON THE BOOB TUBE?
...REMEMBER! REAL LIFE IS NOT A MOVIE!
WHEN YOU ARE BEHIND DA WHEEL, DON'T DRIVE LIKE MCBAIN! DRIVE SAFELY!
SELL OUT! I HATE PUBLIC SERVICE ANNOUNCEMENTS!
"AND NOW BACK TO...EYE ON SPRINGFIELD!"
TONIGHT, WE INVESTIGATE THE WORLD OF THE PAPARAZZI, RUTHLESS CELEBRITY STALKERS WHO HUNT WITH THEIR CAMERAS!
"THE RIGHT SHOT OF A STAR IN AN EMBARRASSING SITUATION CAN BRING IN BIG BUCKS!"
AND I MEAN BOFFO BIG, BERT!
YOU BET, BONNIE!
WHOA! COOL!
SPEAKING OF BOFFO! DUFFMAN WILL BE MAKING A PUBLIC APPEARANCE TOMORROW AT MOE'S TAVERN IN SPRINGFIELD!
DUFFMAN, EH? HE'S A CELEBRITY... SORT OF!

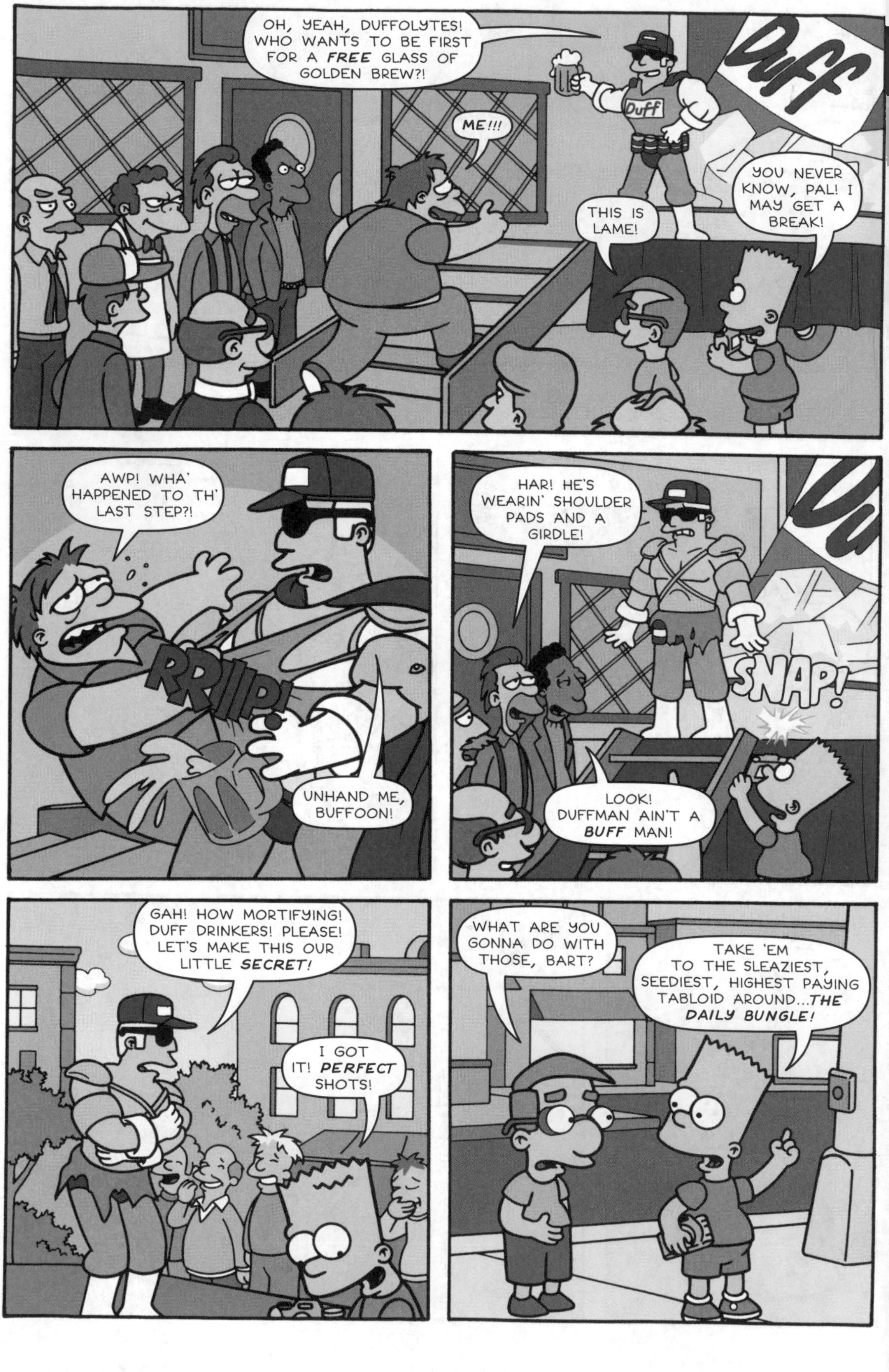
OH, YEAH, DUFFOLYTES! WHO WANTS TO BE FIRST FOR A FREE GLASS OF GOLDEN BREW?!
ME!!!
THIS IS LAME!
YOU NEVER KNOW, PAL! I MAY GET A BREAK!
AWP! WHA' HAPPENED TO TH' LAST STEP?!
RRIIIP!
UNHAND ME, BUFFOON!
HAR! HE'S WEARIN' SHOULDER PADS AND A GIRDLE!
SNAP!
LOOK! DUFFMAN AIN'T A BUFF MAN!
GAH! HOW MORTIFYING! DUFF DRINKERS! PLEASE! LET'S MAKE THIS OUR LITTLE SECRET!
I GOT IT! PERFECT SHOTS!
WHAT ARE YOU GONNA DO WITH THOSE, BART?
TAKE 'EM TO THE SLEAZIEST, SEEDIEST, HIGHEST PAYING TABLOID AROUND...THE DAILY BUNGLE!

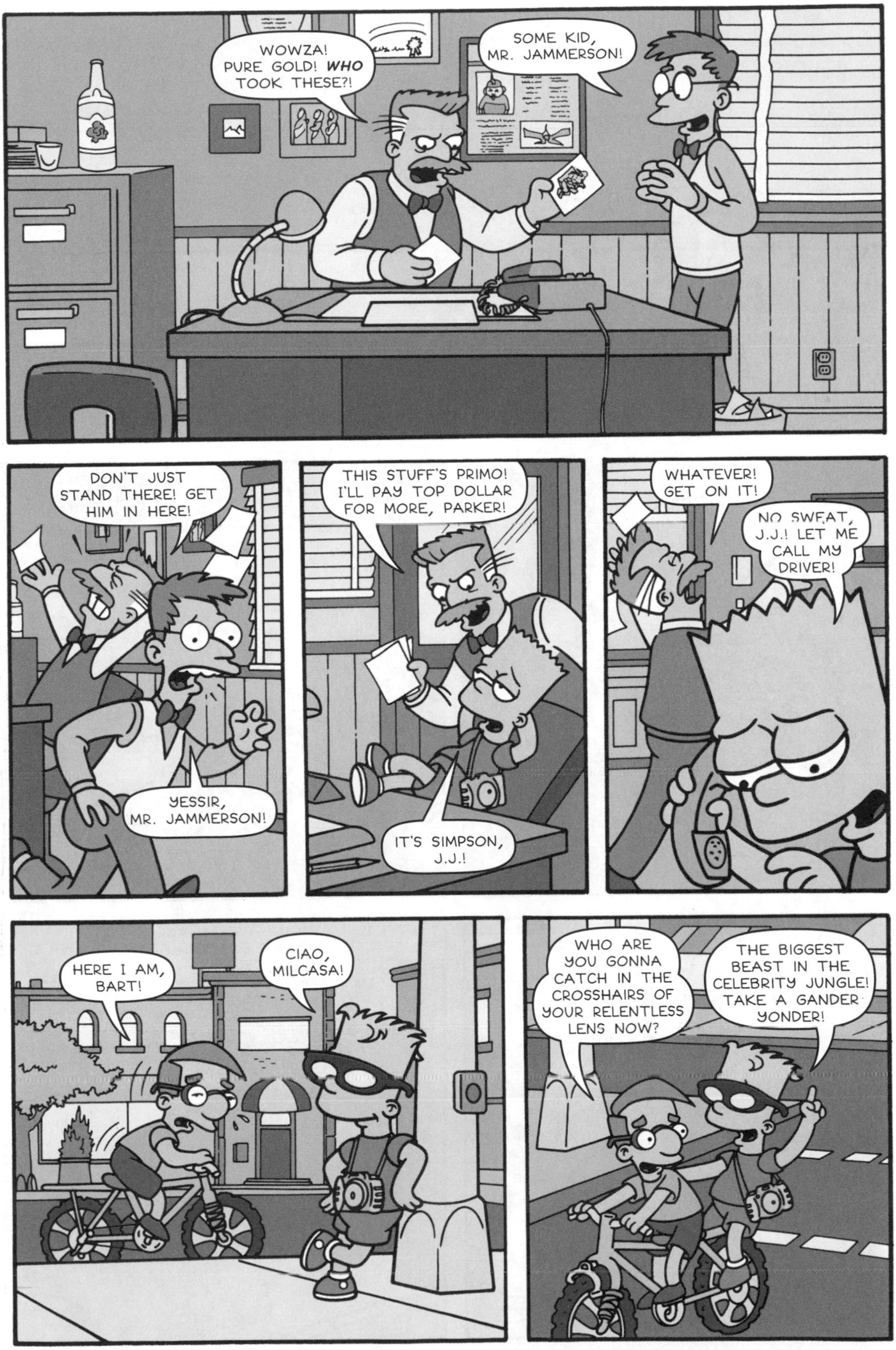
WOWZA! PURE GOLD! **WHO** TOOK THESE?!
SOME KID, MR. JAMMERSON!
DON'T JUST STAND THERE! GET HIM IN HERE!
YESSIR, MR. JAMMERSON!
THIS STUFF'S PRIMO! I'LL PAY TOP DOLLAR FOR MORE, PARKER!
IT'S SIMPSON, J.J.!
WHATEVER! GET ON IT!
NO SWEAT, J.J.! LET ME CALL MY DRIVER!
HERE I AM, BART!
CIAO, MILCASA!
WHO ARE YOU GONNA CATCH IN THE CROSSHAIRS OF YOUR RELENTLESS LENS NOW?
THE BIGGEST BEAST IN THE CELEBRITY JUNGLE! TAKE A GANDER YONDER!

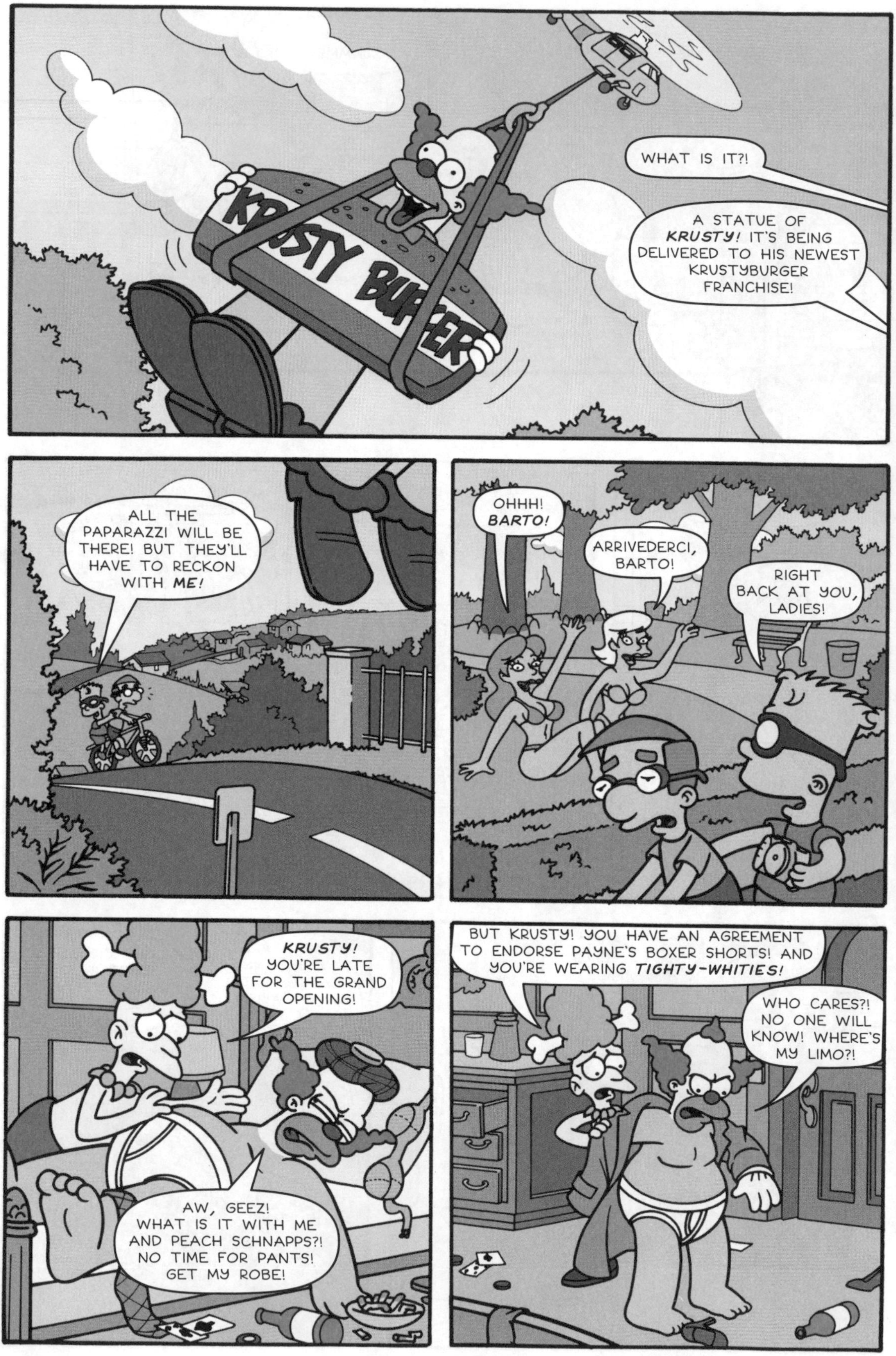
WHAT IS IT?!
A STATUE OF KRUSTY! IT'S BEING DELIVERED TO HIS NEWEST KRUSTYBURGER FRANCHISE!
KRUSTY BURGER
ALL THE PAPARAZZI WILL BE THERE! BUT THEY'LL HAVE TO RECKON WITH ME!
OHHH! BARTO!
ARRIVEDERCI, BARTO!
RIGHT BACK AT YOU, LADIES!
KRUSTY! YOU'RE LATE FOR THE GRAND OPENING!
AW, GEEZ! WHAT IS IT WITH ME AND PEACH SCHNAPPS?! NO TIME FOR PANTS! GET MY ROBE!
BUT KRUSTY! YOU HAVE AN AGREEMENT TO ENDORSE PAYNE'S BOXER SHORTS! AND YOU'RE WEARING TIGHTY-WHITIES!
WHO CARES?! NO ONE WILL KNOW! WHERE'S MY LIMO?!

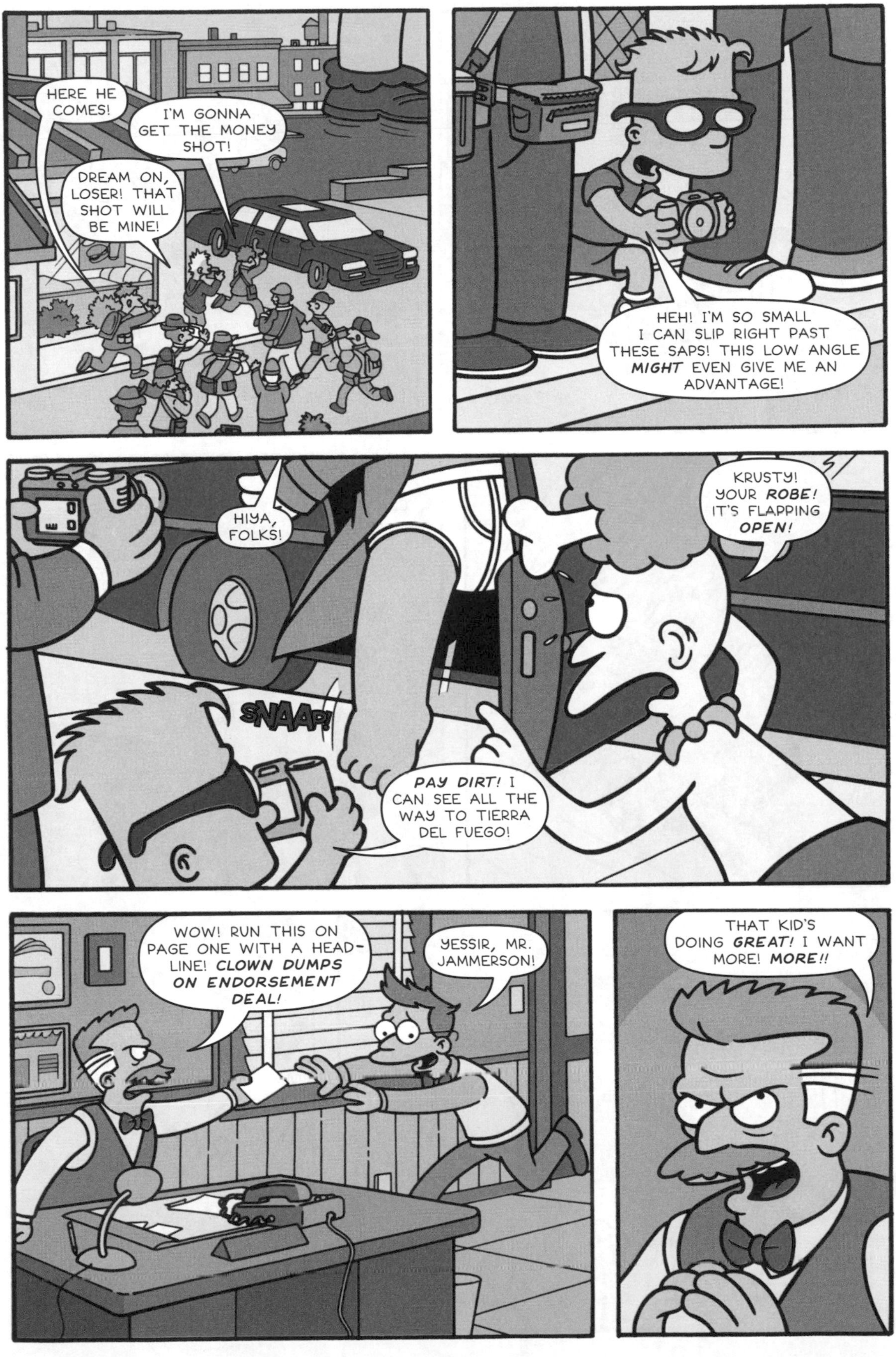
HERE HE COMES!
I'M GONNA GET THE MONEY SHOT!
DREAM ON, LOSER! THAT SHOT WILL BE MINE!
HEH! I'M SO SMALL I CAN SLIP RIGHT PAST THESE SAPS! THIS LOW ANGLE ***MIGHT*** EVEN GIVE ME AN ADVANTAGE!
HIYA, FOLKS!
KRUSTY! YOUR ***ROBE***! IT'S FLAPPING ***OPEN***!
SNAAP!
PAY DIRT! I CAN SEE ALL THE WAY TO TIERRA DEL FUEGO!
WOW! RUN THIS ON PAGE ONE WITH A HEAD-LINE! ***CLOWN DUMPS ON ENDORSEMENT DEAL***!
YESSIR, MR. JAMMERSON!
THAT KID'S DOING ***GREAT***! I WANT MORE! ***MORE***!!

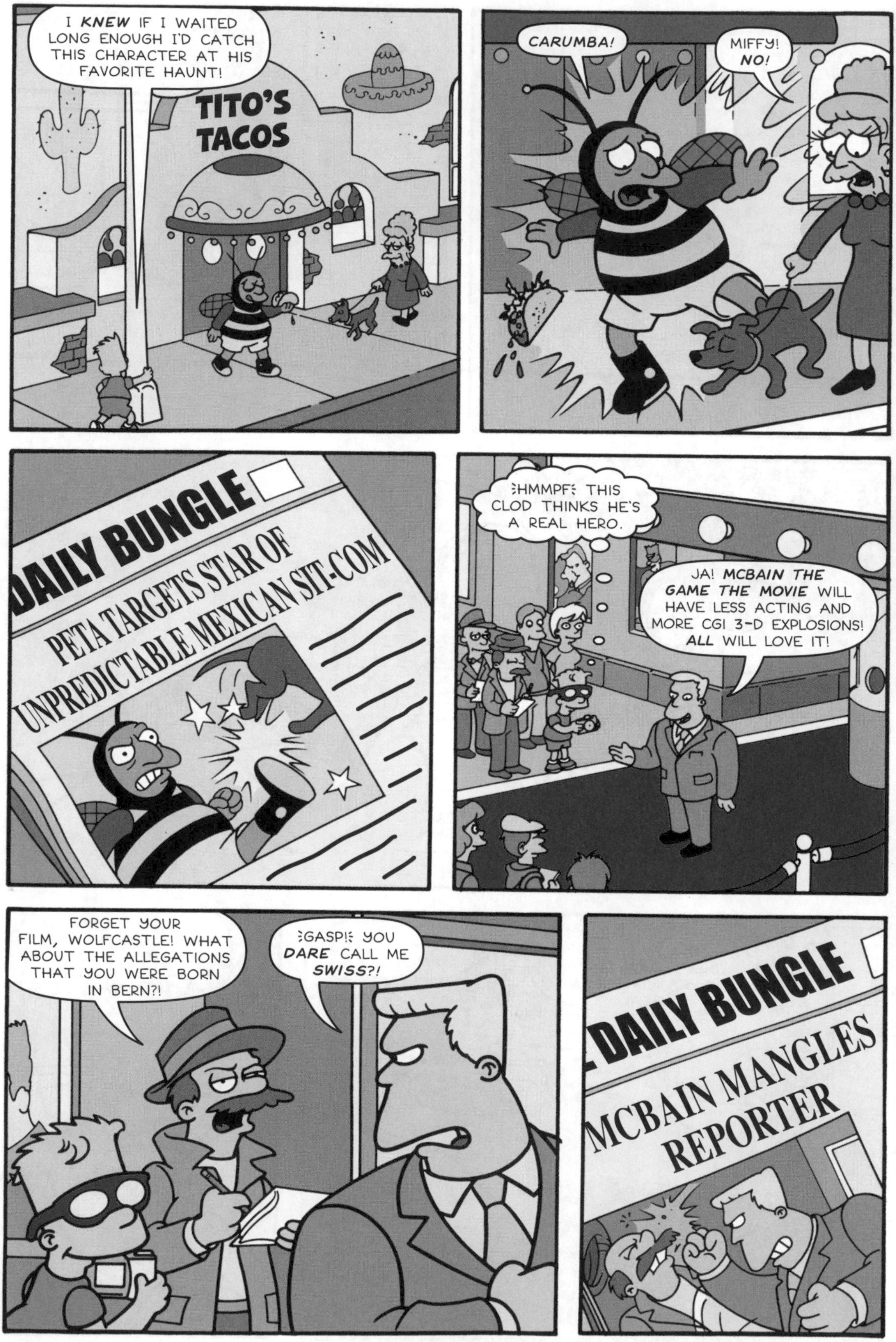
I KNEW IF I WAITED LONG ENOUGH I'D CATCH THIS CHARACTER AT HIS FAVORITE HAUNT!
TITO'S TACOS
CARUMBA!
MIFFY! NO!
DAILY BUNGLE
PETA TARGETS STAR OF UNPREDICTABLE MEXICAN SIT-COM
HMMPF THIS CLOD THINKS HE'S A REAL HERO.
JA! MCBAIN THE GAME THE MOVIE WILL HAVE LESS ACTING AND MORE CGI 3-D EXPLOSIONS! ALL WILL LOVE IT!
FORGET YOUR FILM, WOLFCASTLE! WHAT ABOUT THE ALLEGATIONS THAT YOU WERE BORN IN BERN?!
GASP! YOU DARE CALL ME SWISS?!
DAILY BUNGLE
MCBAIN MANGLES REPORTER

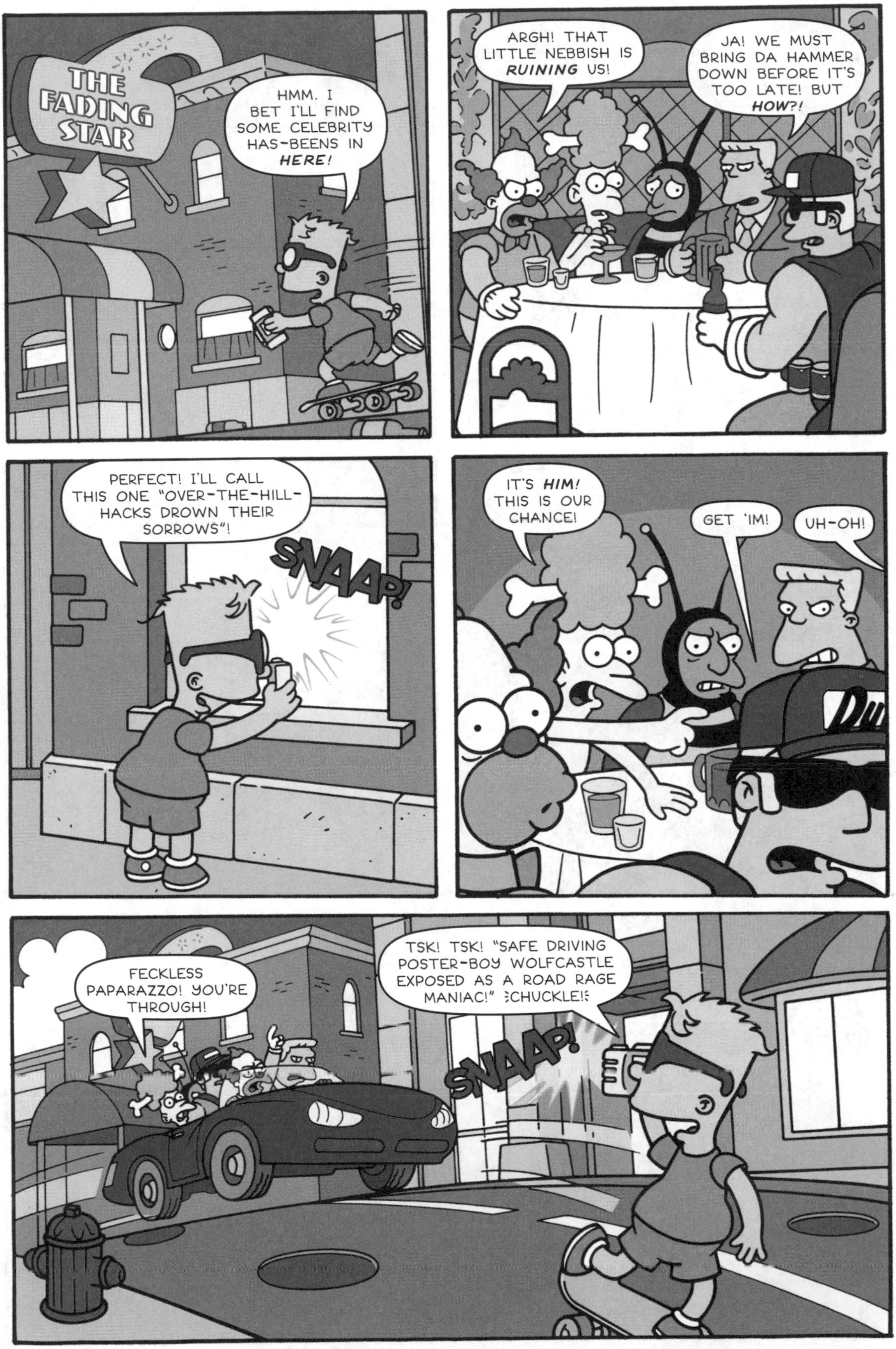
THE FADING STAR
HMM. I BET I'LL FIND SOME CELEBRITY HAS-BEENS IN HERE!
ARGH! THAT LITTLE NEBBISH IS RUINING US!
JA! WE MUST BRING DA HAMMER DOWN BEFORE IT'S TOO LATE! BUT HOW?!
PERFECT! I'LL CALL THIS ONE "OVER-THE-HILL-HACKS DROWN THEIR SORROWS"!
SNAAP!
IT'S HIM! THIS IS OUR CHANCE!
GET 'IM!
UH-OH!
FECKLESS PAPARAZZO! YOU'RE THROUGH!
TSK! TSK! "SAFE DRIVING POSTER-BOY WOLFCASTLE EXPOSED AS A ROAD RAGE MANIAC!" ⁝CHUCKLE!⁝
SNAAP!

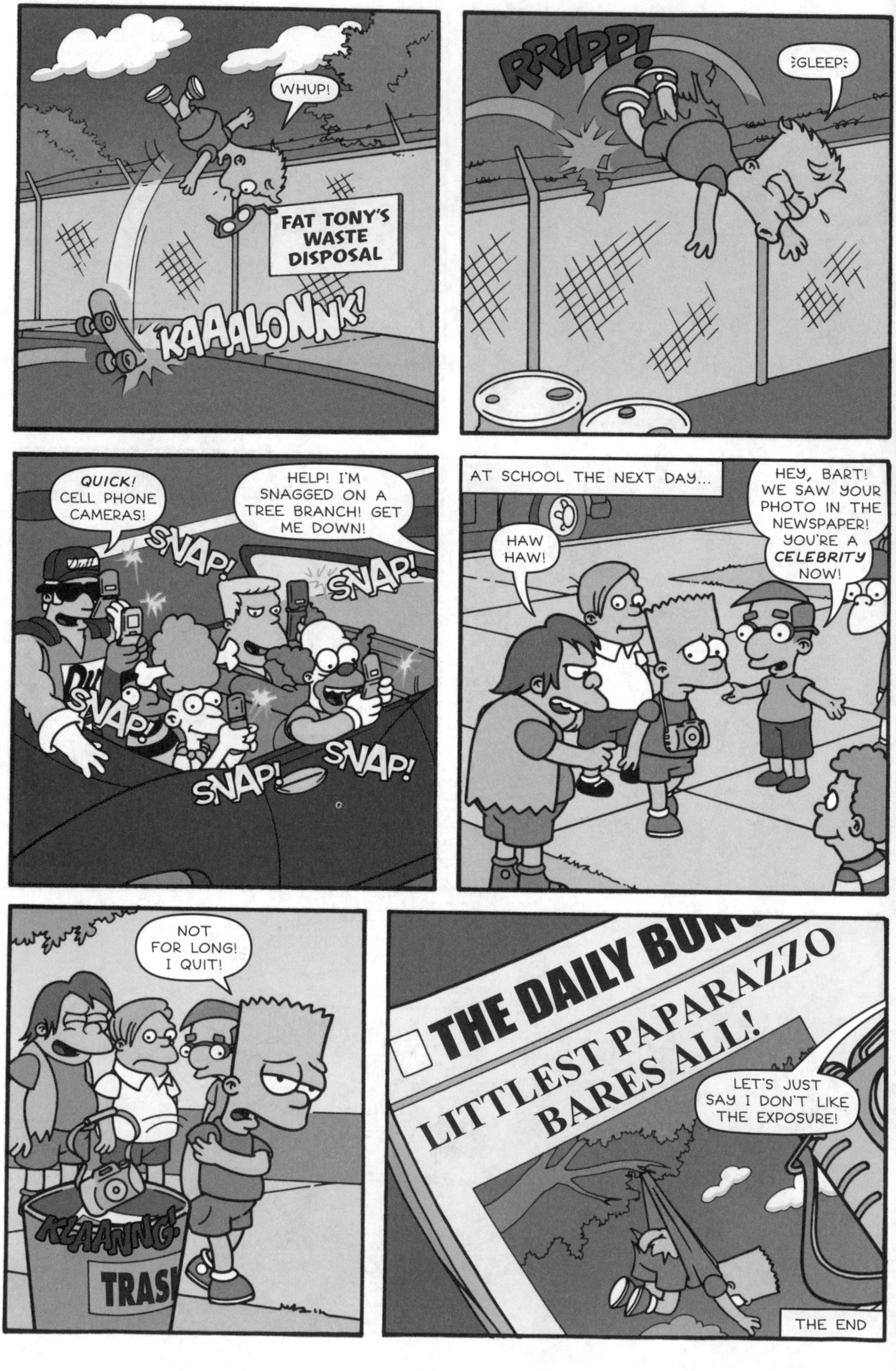
WHUP!
FAT TONY'S WASTE DISPOSAL
KAAALONNK!
RRIIPP!
GLEEP
QUICK! CELL PHONE CAMERAS!
HELP! I'M SNAGGED ON A TREE BRANCH! GET ME DOWN!
SNAP!
SNAP!
SNAP!
SNAP!
SNAP!
AT SCHOOL THE NEXT DAY...
HAW HAW!
HEY, BART! WE SAW YOUR PHOTO IN THE NEWSPAPER! YOU'RE A CELEBRITY NOW!
NOT FOR LONG! I QUIT!
KLAANNG!
TRAS
THE DAILY BUN
LITTLEST PAPARAZZO BARES ALL!
LET'S JUST SAY I DON'T LIKE THE EXPOSURE!
THE END

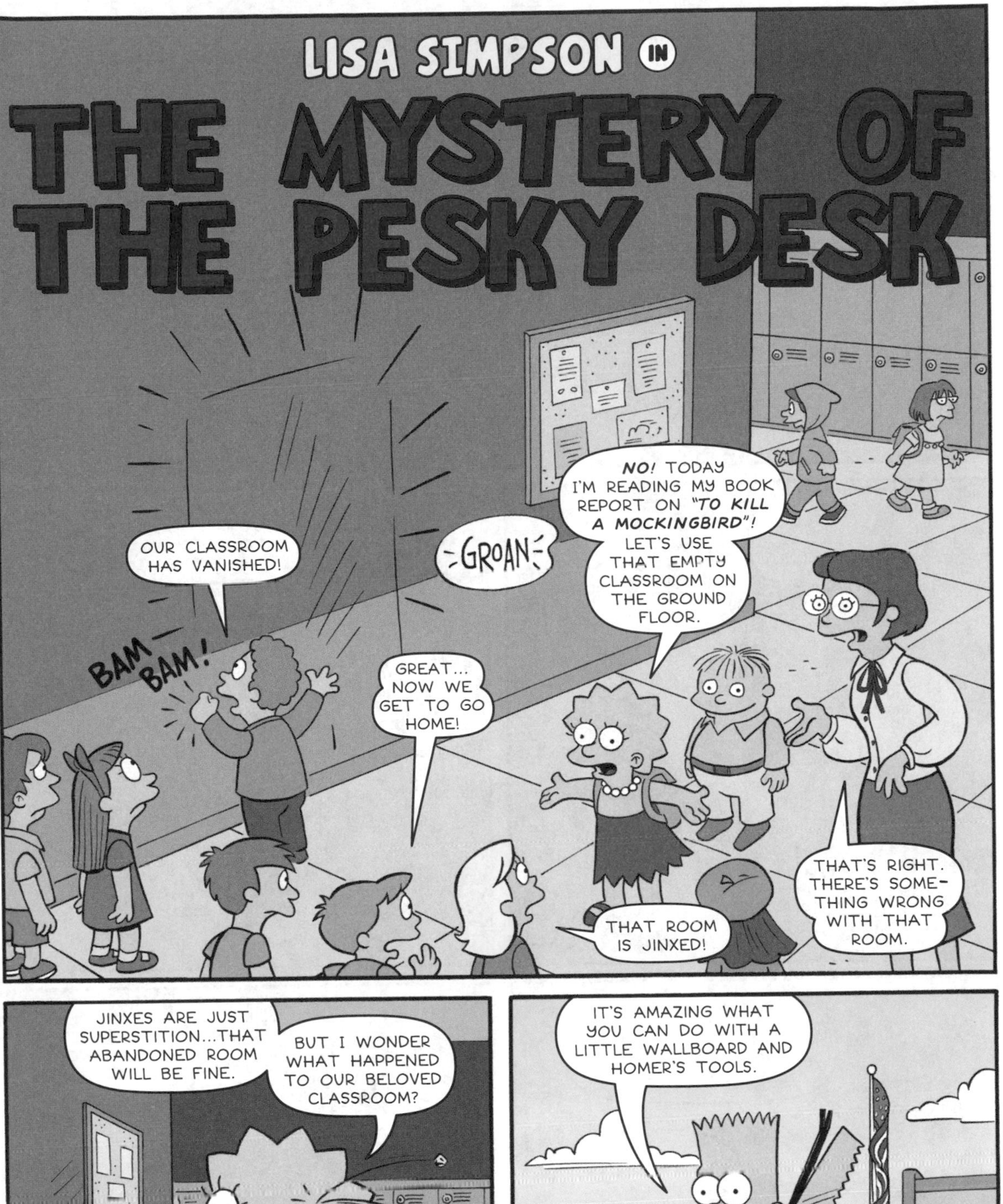
LISA SIMPSON IN
THE MYSTERY OF THE PESKY DESK
OUR CLASSROOM HAS VANISHED!
BAM BAM!
GROAN
NO! TODAY I'M READING MY BOOK REPORT ON "TO KILL A MOCKINGBIRD"! LET'S USE THAT EMPTY CLASSROOM ON THE GROUND FLOOR.
GREAT... NOW WE GET TO GO HOME!
THAT ROOM IS JINXED!
THAT'S RIGHT. THERE'S SOME-THING WRONG WITH THAT ROOM.
JINXES ARE JUST SUPERSTITION...THAT ABANDONED ROOM WILL BE FINE.
BUT I WONDER WHAT HAPPENED TO OUR BELOVED CLASSROOM?
PING!
MATT GROENING
IT'S AMAZING WHAT YOU CAN DO WITH A LITTLE WALLBOARD AND HOMER'S TOOLS.

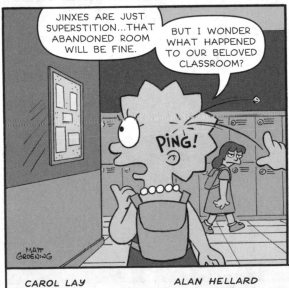

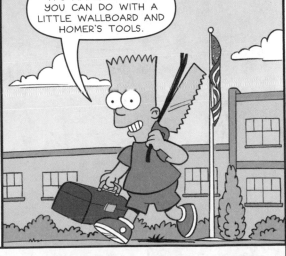

CAROL LAY STORY & ART | **ALAN HELLARD** COLORS | **KAREN BATES** LETTERS | **BILL MORRISON** EDITOR

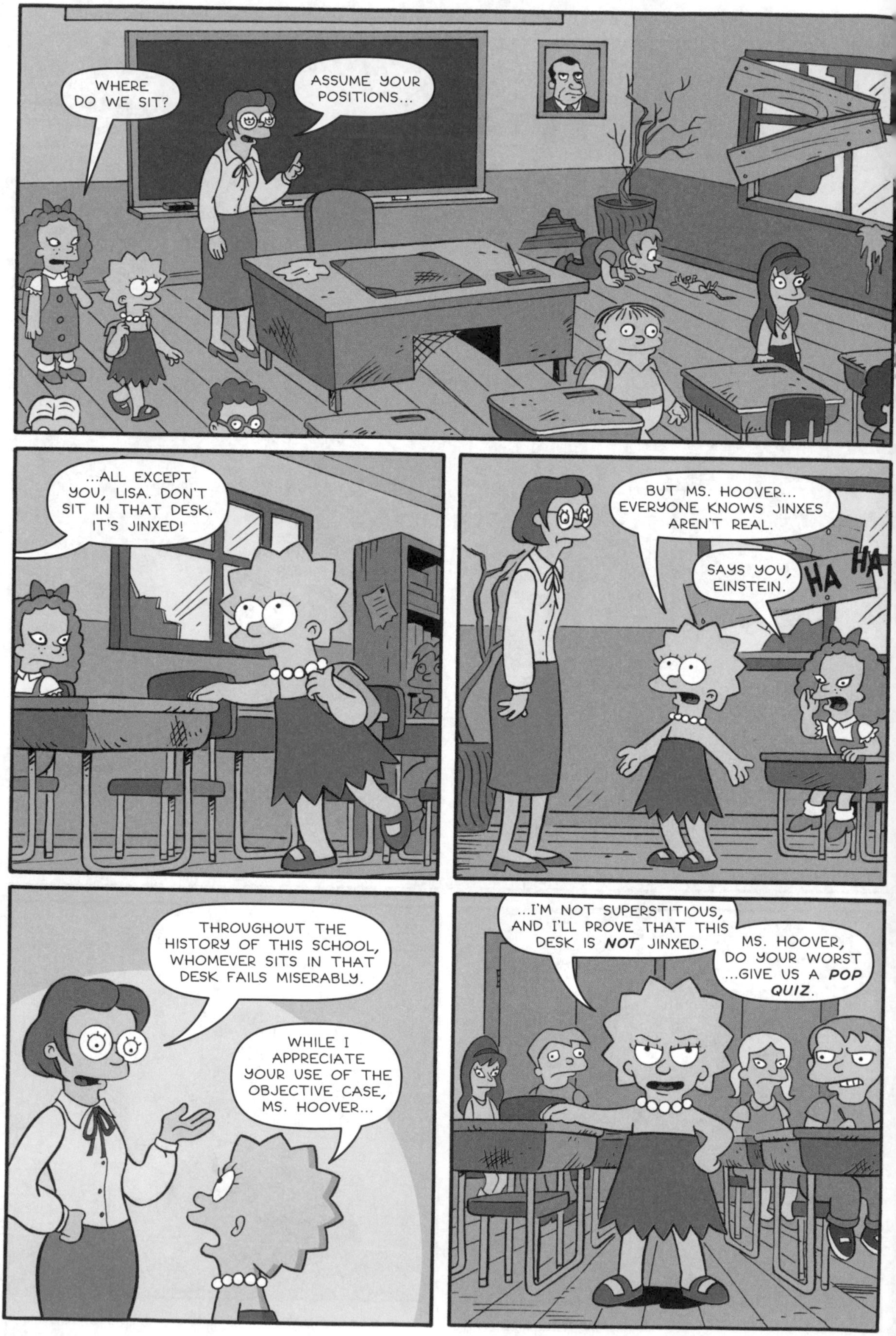
WHERE DO WE SIT?
ASSUME YOUR POSITIONS...
...ALL EXCEPT YOU, LISA. DON'T SIT IN THAT DESK. IT'S JINXED!
BUT MS. HOOVER... EVERYONE KNOWS JINXES AREN'T REAL.
SAYS YOU, EINSTEIN.
HA HA
THROUGHOUT THE HISTORY OF THIS SCHOOL, WHOMEVER SITS IN THAT DESK FAILS MISERABLY.
WHILE I APPRECIATE YOUR USE OF THE OBJECTIVE CASE, MS. HOOVER...
...I'M NOT SUPERSTITIOUS, AND I'LL PROVE THAT THIS DESK IS NOT JINXED.
MS. HOOVER, DO YOUR WORST ...GIVE US A POP QUIZ.

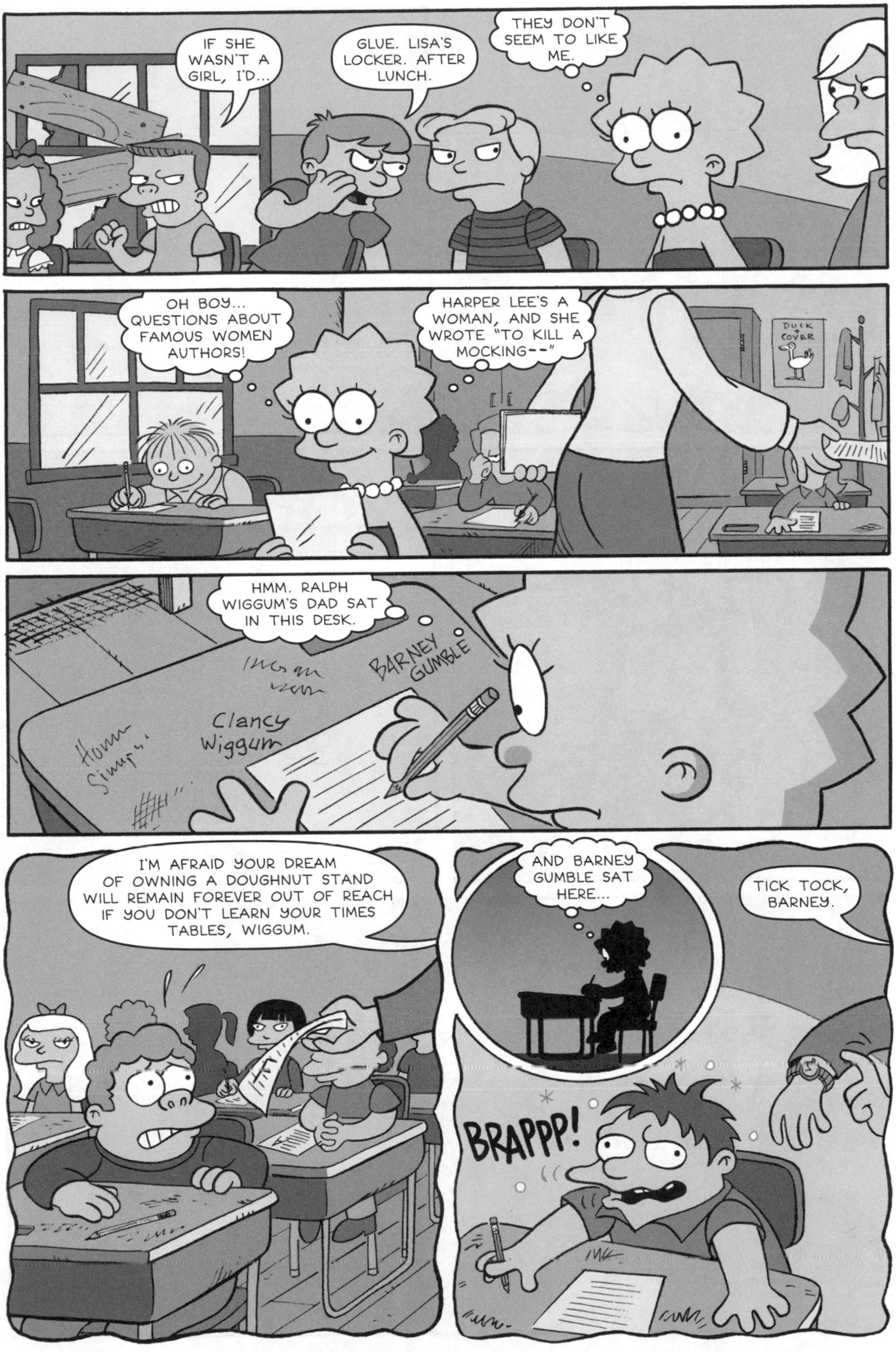
IF SHE WASN'T A GIRL, I'D...
GLUE. LISA'S LOCKER. AFTER LUNCH.
THEY DON'T SEEM TO LIKE ME.
OH BOY... QUESTIONS ABOUT FAMOUS WOMEN AUTHORS!
HARPER LEE'S A WOMAN, AND SHE WROTE "TO KILL A MOCKING--"
DUCK + COVER
HMM. RALPH WIGGUM'S DAD SAT IN THIS DESK.
BARNEY GUMBLE
Clancy Wiggum
I'M AFRAID YOUR DREAM OF OWNING A DOUGHNUT STAND WILL REMAIN FOREVER OUT OF REACH IF YOU DON'T LEARN YOUR TIMES TABLES, WIGGUM.
AND BARNEY GUMBLE SAT HERE...
TICK TOCK, BARNEY.
BRAPPP!

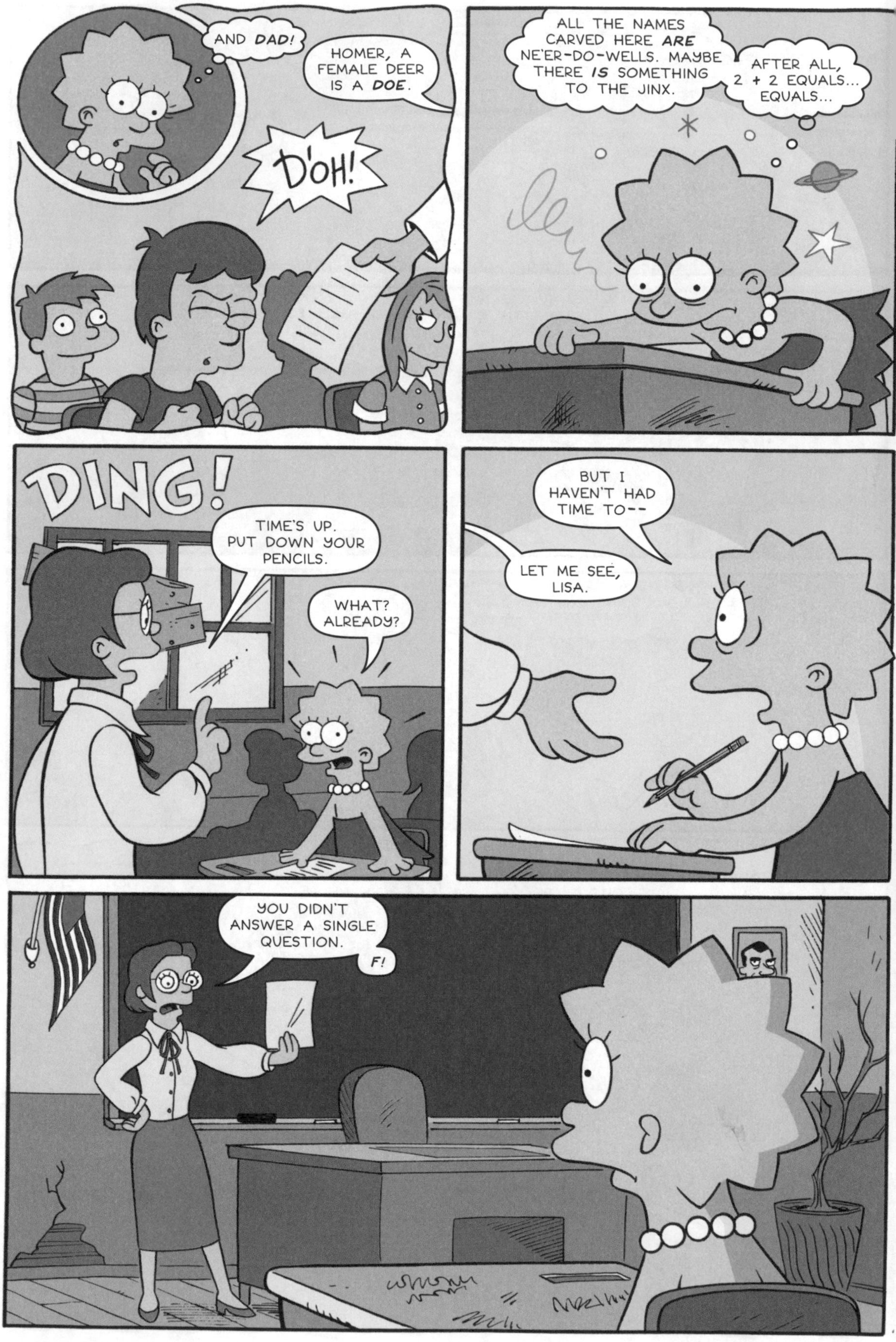

AND DAD!
HOMER, A FEMALE DEER IS A DOE.
D'OH!
ALL THE NAMES CARVED HERE ARE NE'ER-DO-WELLS. MAYBE THERE IS SOMETHING TO THE JINX.
AFTER ALL, 2 + 2 EQUALS... EQUALS...
DING!
TIME'S UP. PUT DOWN YOUR PENCILS.
WHAT? ALREADY?
BUT I HAVEN'T HAD TIME TO--
LET ME SEE, LISA.
YOU DIDN'T ANSWER A SINGLE QUESTION.
F!

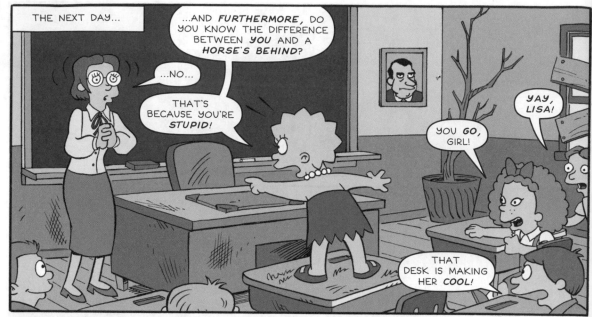

THE NEXT DAY...

...AND *FURTHERMORE*, DO YOU KNOW THE DIFFERENCE BETWEEN *YOU* AND A *HORSE'S BEHIND*?

...NO...

THAT'S BECAUSE YOU'RE *STUPID*!

YAY, LISA!

YOU *GO*, GIRL!

THAT DESK IS MAKING HER *COOL*!

I'M *BLOWING* THIS *POP STAND*! I SUDDENLY FEEL THE URGE TO GET SOME *TATTOOS* AND A *LEATHER JACKET*.

SOUNDS *HOT*!

HA HA!

I *CAN'T BELIEVE* HOW IDIOTIC ALL THOSE... THOSE...

WOW. THIS *FRESH AIR* IS RESTORING MY MENTAL FACULTIES!

AND THAT GIVES ME AN IDEA ON HOW I CAN SOLVE THIS MYSTERY!

I HOPE MOM DIDN'T THROW OUT MY SCIENCE PROJECT FROM LAST YEAR!

SPRINGFIELD ELEMENTARY SCHOOL

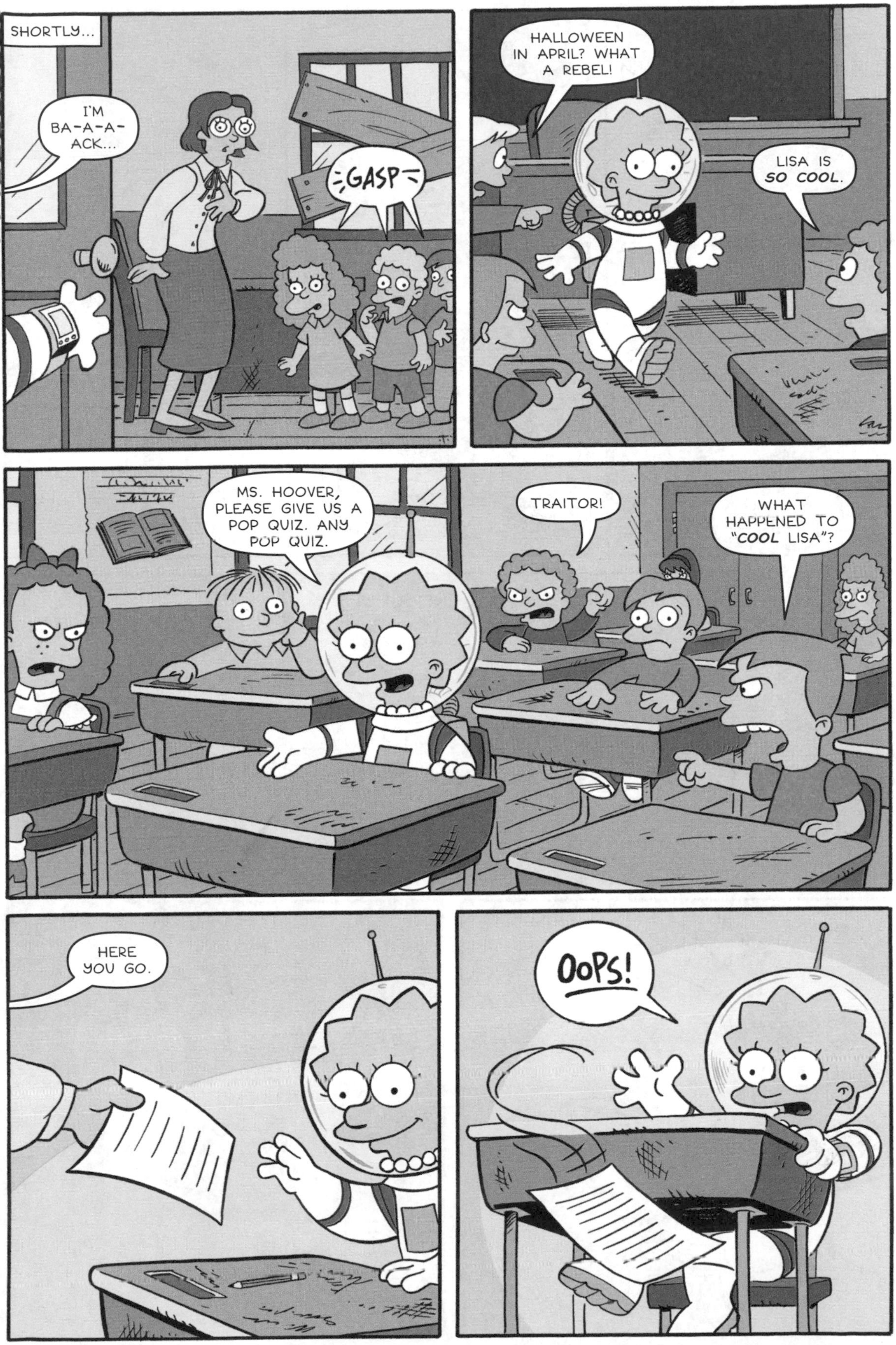
SHORTLY...
I'M BA-A-A-ACK...
GASP
HALLOWEEN IN APRIL? WHAT A REBEL!
LISA IS SO COOL.
MS. HOOVER, PLEASE GIVE US A POP QUIZ. ANY POP QUIZ.
TRAITOR!
WHAT HAPPENED TO "COOL LISA"?
HERE YOU GO.
OOPS!

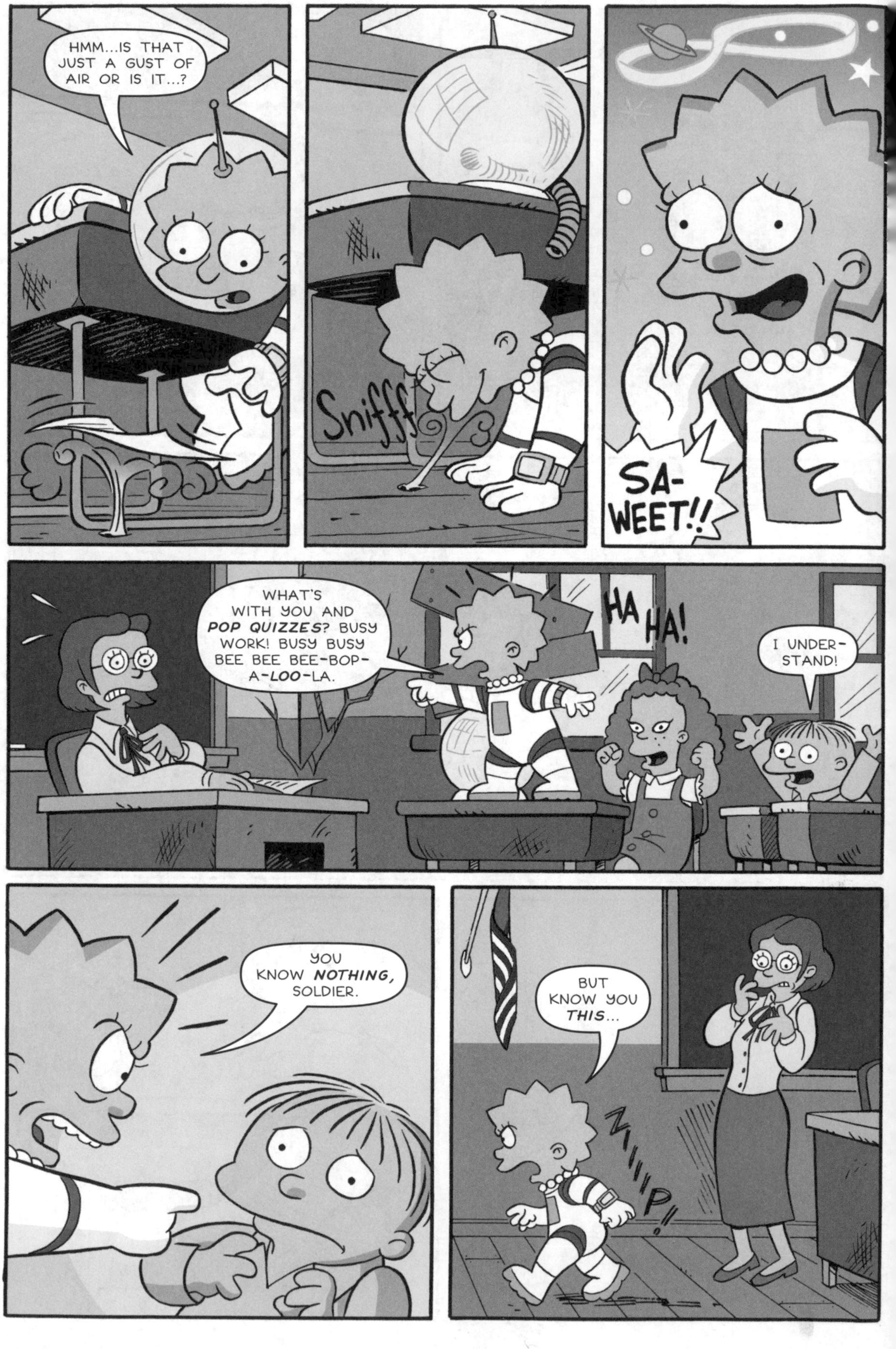
HMM...IS THAT JUST A GUST OF AIR OR IS IT...?
Snifff
SA-WEET!!
WHAT'S WITH YOU AND ***POP QUIZZES***? BUSY WORK! BUSY BUSY BEE BEE BEE-BOP-A-***LOO***-LA.
HA HA!
I UNDER-STAND!
YOU KNOW ***NOTHING,*** SOLDIER.
BUT KNOW YOU ***THIS***...
ZIIIP!!

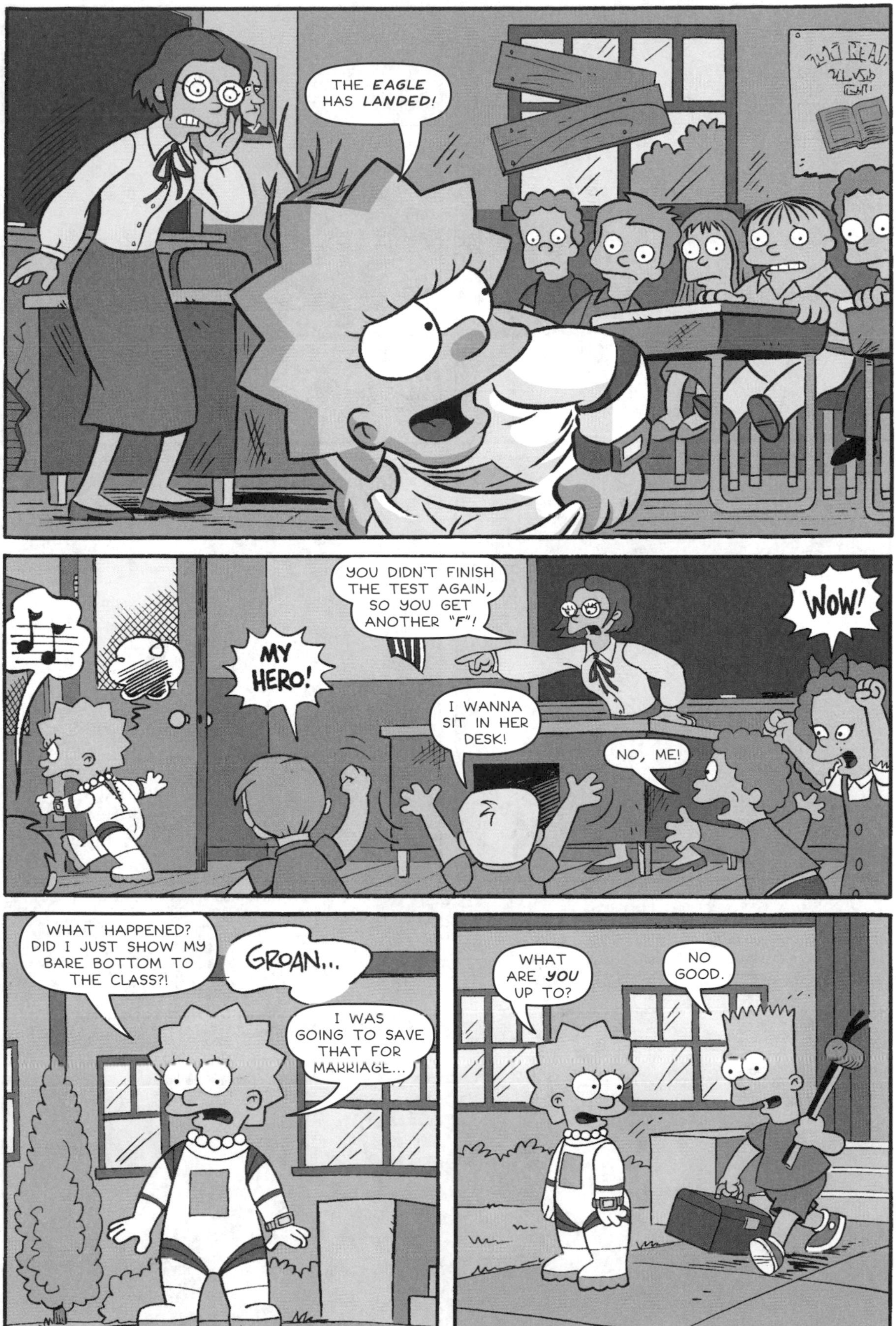
THE EAGLE HAS LANDED!
YOU DIDN'T FINISH THE TEST AGAIN, SO YOU GET ANOTHER "F"!
MY HERO!
WOW!
I WANNA SIT IN HER DESK!
NO, ME!
WHAT HAPPENED? DID I JUST SHOW MY BARE BOTTOM TO THE CLASS?!
GROAN...
I WAS GOING TO SAVE THAT FOR MARRIAGE...
WHAT ARE YOU UP TO?
NO GOOD.

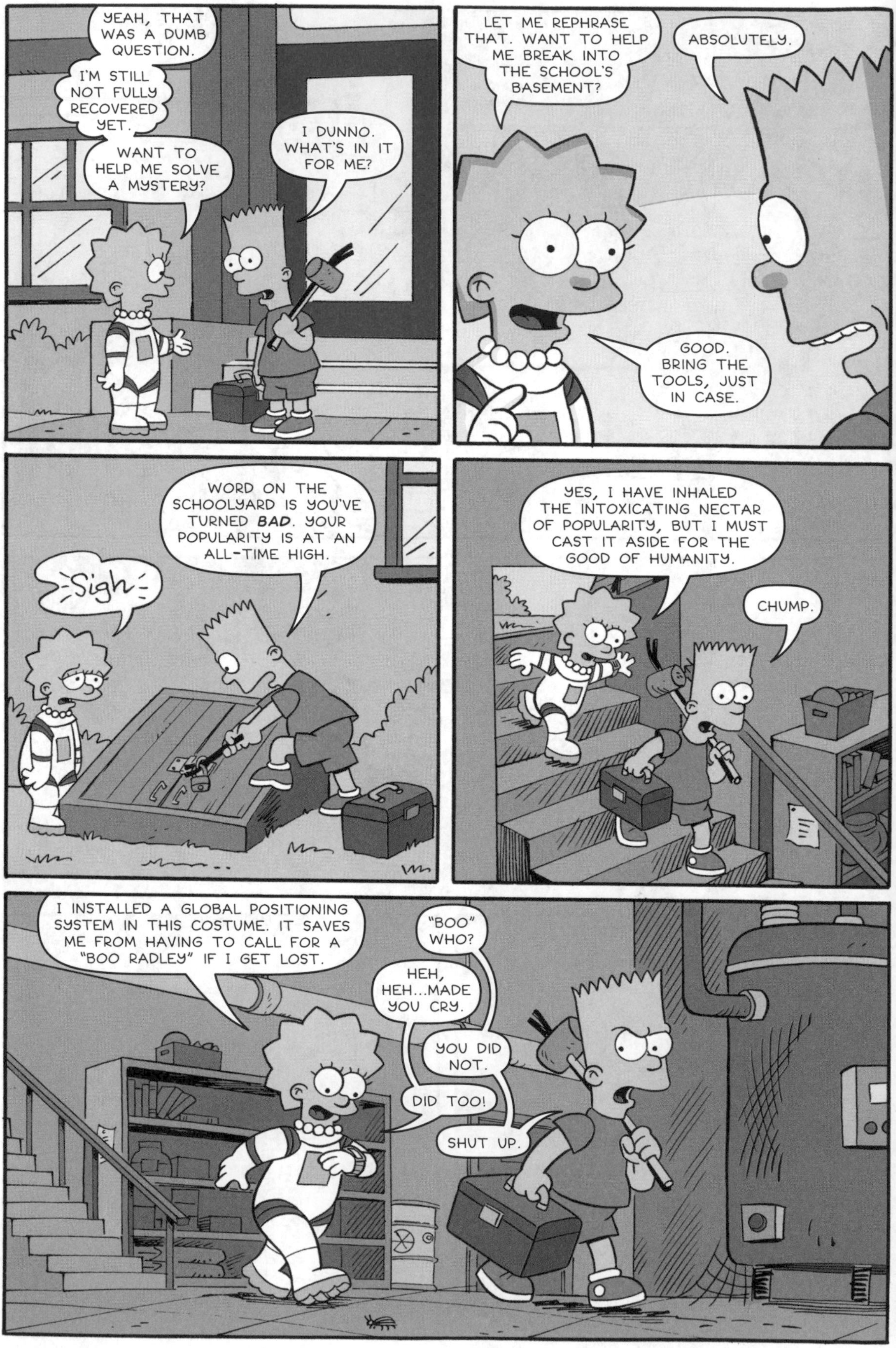
YEAH, THAT WAS A DUMB QUESTION.
I'M STILL NOT FULLY RECOVERED YET.
WANT TO HELP ME SOLVE A MYSTERY?
I DUNNO. WHAT'S IN IT FOR ME?
LET ME REPHRASE THAT. WANT TO HELP ME BREAK INTO THE SCHOOL'S BASEMENT?
ABSOLUTELY.
GOOD. BRING THE TOOLS, JUST IN CASE.
WORD ON THE SCHOOLYARD IS YOU'VE TURNED **BAD**. YOUR POPULARITY IS AT AN ALL-TIME HIGH.
Sigh
YES, I HAVE INHALED THE INTOXICATING NECTAR OF POPULARITY, BUT I MUST CAST IT ASIDE FOR THE GOOD OF HUMANITY.
CHUMP.
I INSTALLED A GLOBAL POSITIONING SYSTEM IN THIS COSTUME. IT SAVES ME FROM HAVING TO CALL FOR A "BOO RADLEY" IF I GET LOST.
"BOO" WHO?
HEH, HEH...MADE YOU CRY.
YOU DID NOT.
DID TOO!
SHUT UP.

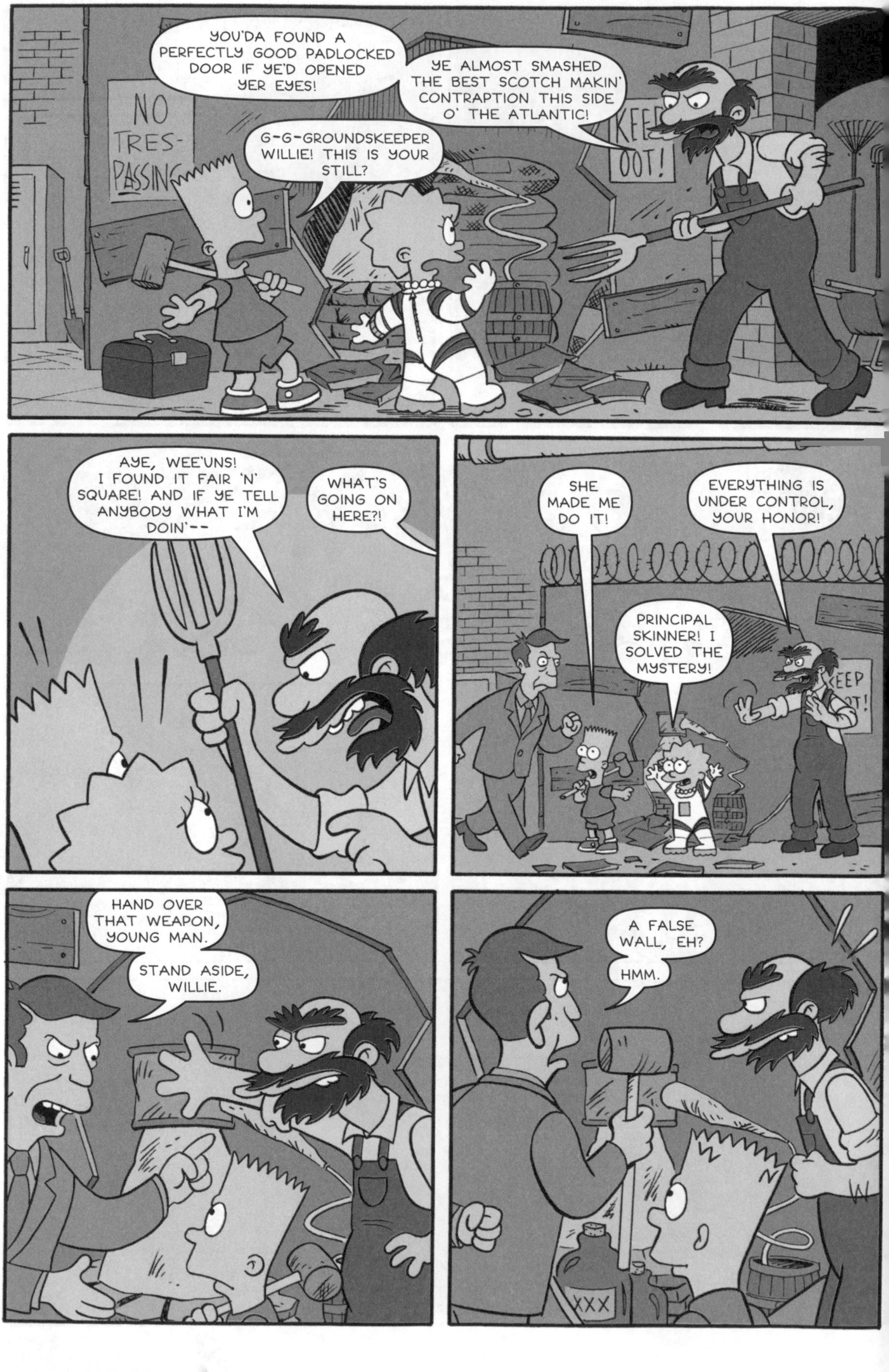

YOU'DA FOUND A PERFECTLY GOOD PADLOCKED DOOR IF YE'D OPENED YER EYES!
YE ALMOST SMASHED THE BEST SCOTCH MAKIN' CONTRAPTION THIS SIDE O' THE ATLANTIC!
NO TRES-PASSING
KEEP OOT!
G-G-GROUNDSKEEPER WILLIE! THIS IS YOUR STILL?
AYE, WEE'UNS! I FOUND IT FAIR 'N' SQUARE! AND IF YE TELL ANYBODY WHAT I'M DOIN'--
WHAT'S GOING ON HERE?!
SHE MADE ME DO IT!
EVERYTHING IS UNDER CONTROL, YOUR HONOR!
PRINCIPAL SKINNER! I SOLVED THE MYSTERY!
HAND OVER THAT WEAPON, YOUNG MAN.
STAND ASIDE, WILLIE.
A FALSE WALL, EH?
HMM.
XXX

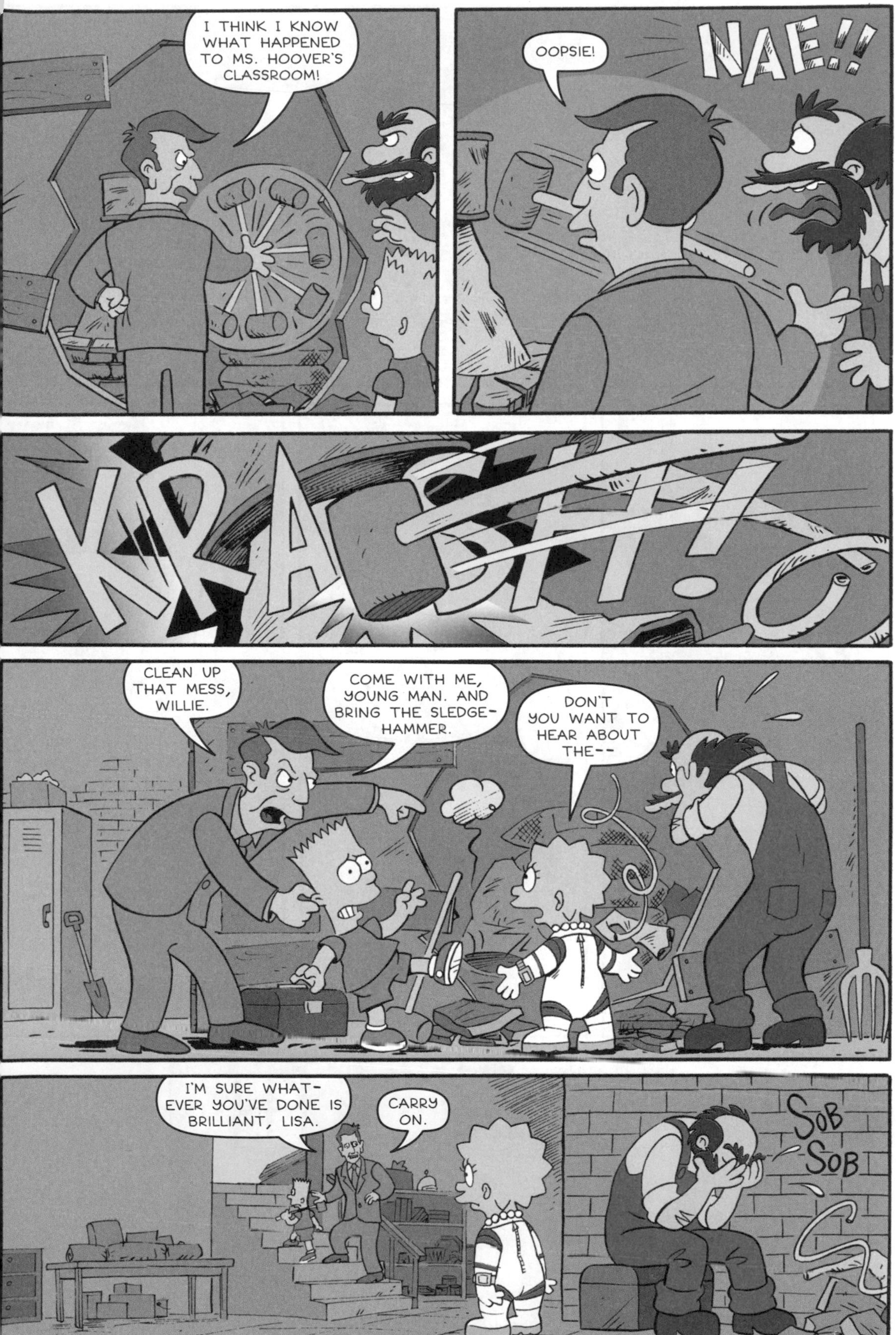

I THINK I KNOW WHAT HAPPENED TO MS. HOOVER'S CLASSROOM!
OOPSIE!
NAE!!
KRASH!
CLEAN UP THAT MESS, WILLIE.
COME WITH ME, YOUNG MAN. AND BRING THE SLEDGE-HAMMER.
DON'T YOU WANT TO HEAR ABOUT THE--
I'M SURE WHAT-EVER YOU'VE DONE IS BRILLIANT, LISA.
CARRY ON.
SOB SOB

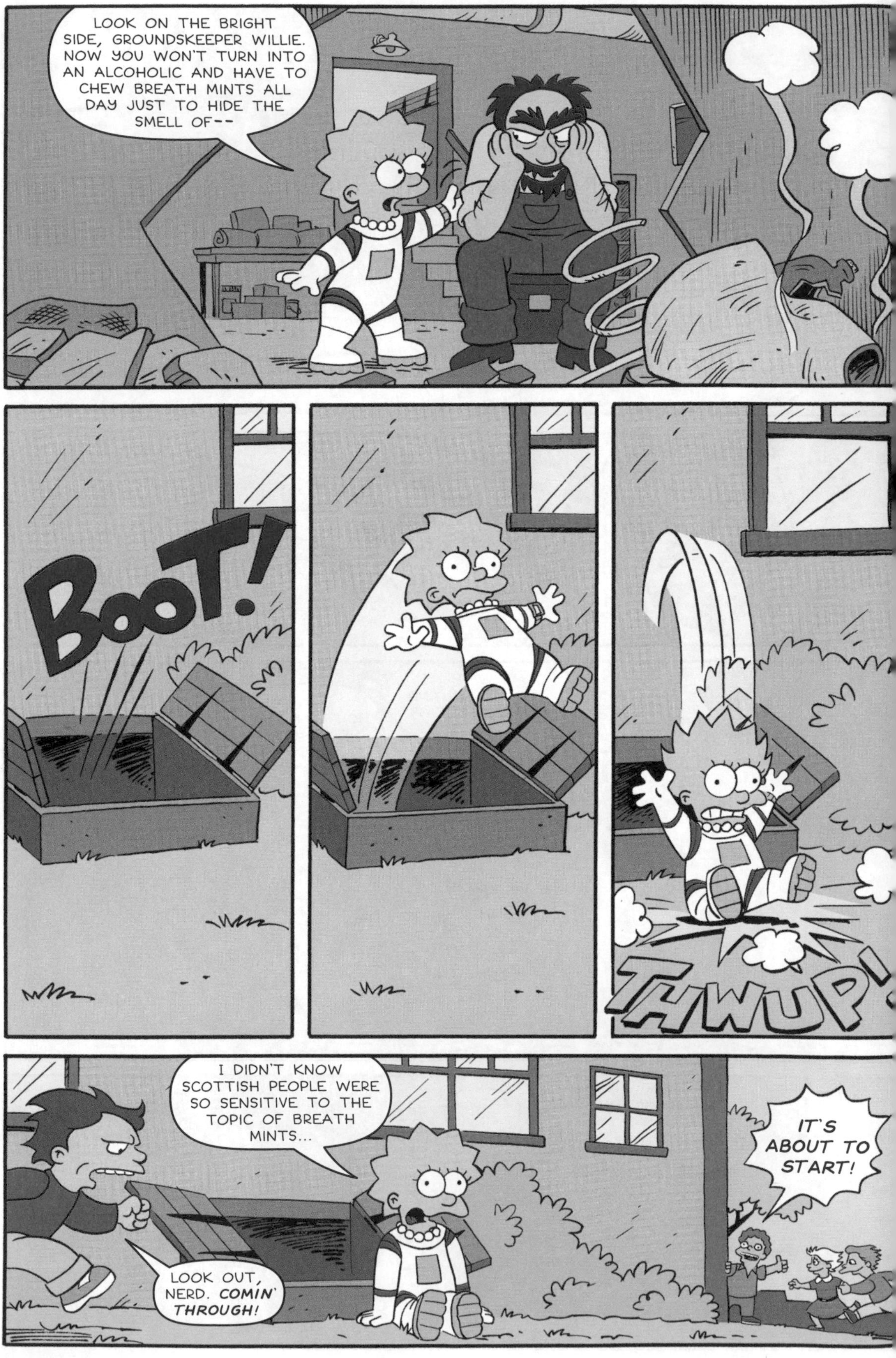
LOOK ON THE BRIGHT SIDE, GROUNDSKEEPER WILLIE. NOW YOU WON'T TURN INTO AN ALCOHOLIC AND HAVE TO CHEW BREATH MINTS ALL DAY JUST TO HIDE THE SMELL OF--
BOOT!
THWUP!
I DIDN'T KNOW SCOTTISH PEOPLE WERE SO SENSITIVE TO THE TOPIC OF BREATH MINTS...
LOOK OUT, NERD. COMIN' THROUGH!
IT'S ABOUT TO START!

THE END

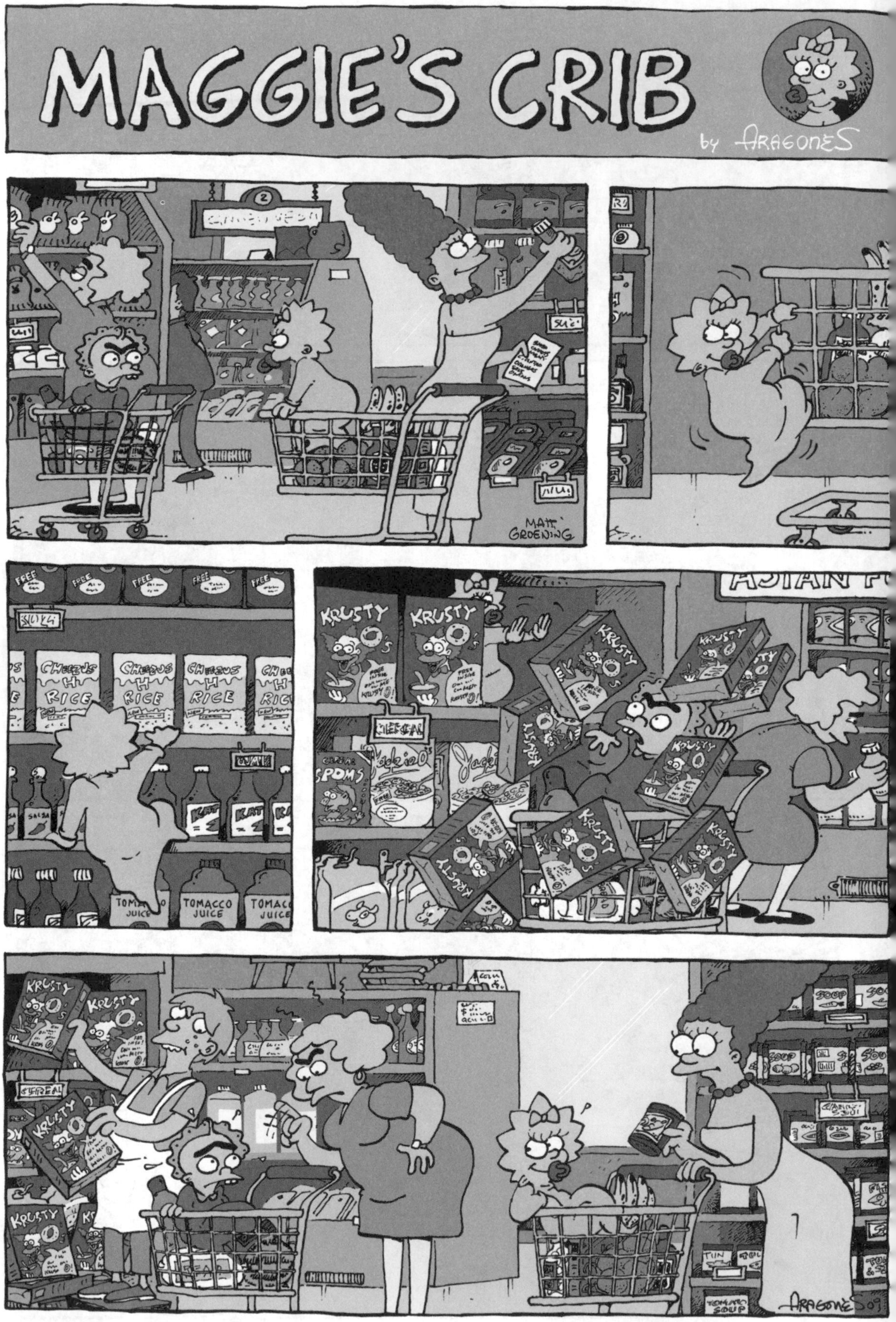
MAGGIE'S CRIB
by ARAGONES
MATT GROENING
KRUSTY O's
CHEEZUS H RICE
SALSA
SPOMS
TOMACCO JUICE
KRUSTY
SOUP
TOMATO SOUP
ARAGONÉS 09

SERGIO ARAGONÉS
STORY & ART

ART VILLANUEVA
COLORS

BILL MORRISON
EDITOR

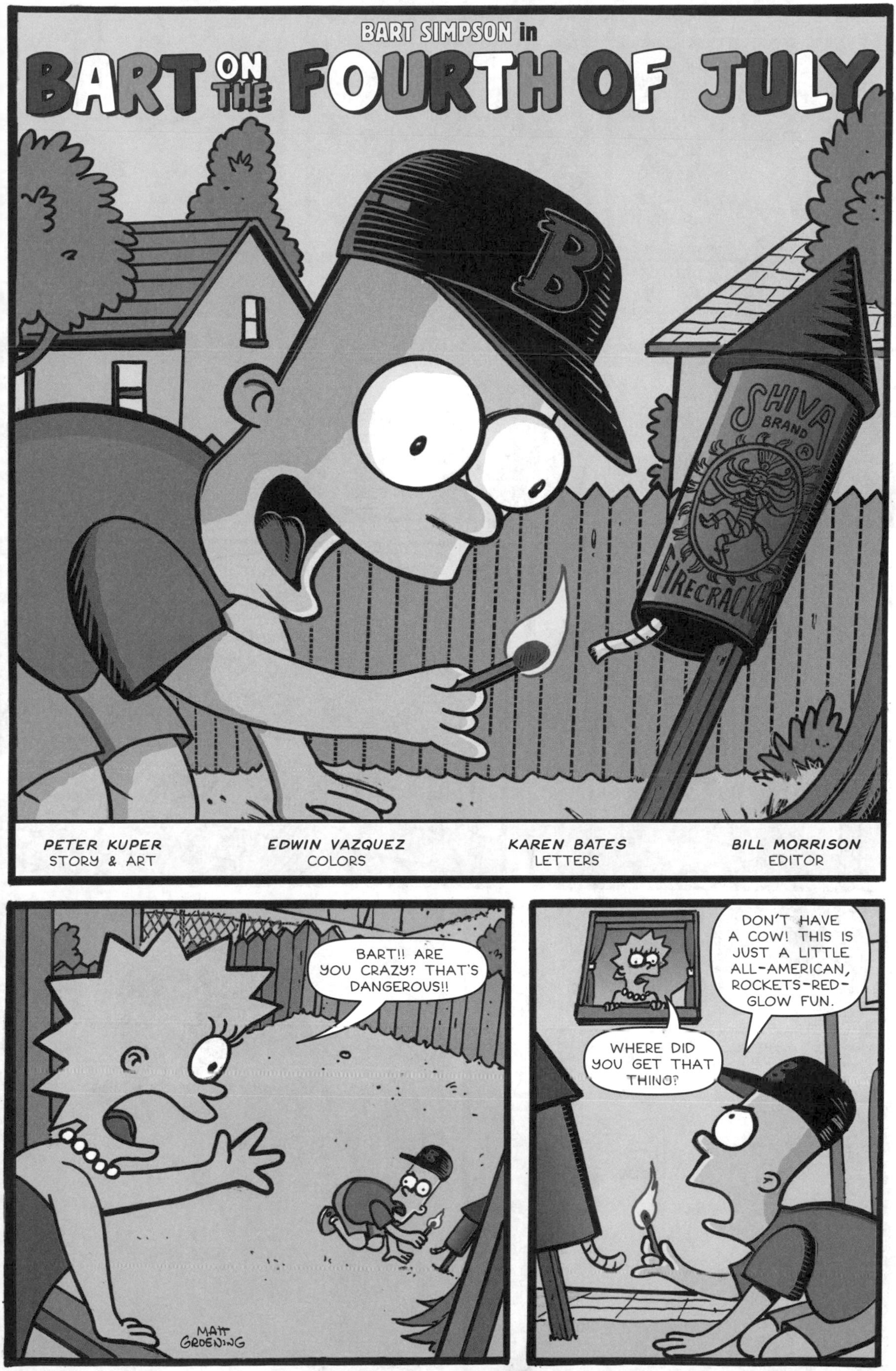
BART SIMPSON in
BART ON THE FOURTH OF JULY
SHIVA BRAND
FIRECRACKER
PETER KUPER STORY & ART
EDWIN VAZQUEZ COLORS
KAREN BATES LETTERS
BILL MORRISON EDITOR
BART!! ARE YOU CRAZY? THAT'S DANGEROUS!!
MATT GROENING
DON'T HAVE A COW! THIS IS JUST A LITTLE ALL-AMERICAN, ROCKETS-RED-GLOW FUN.
WHERE DID YOU GET THAT THING?

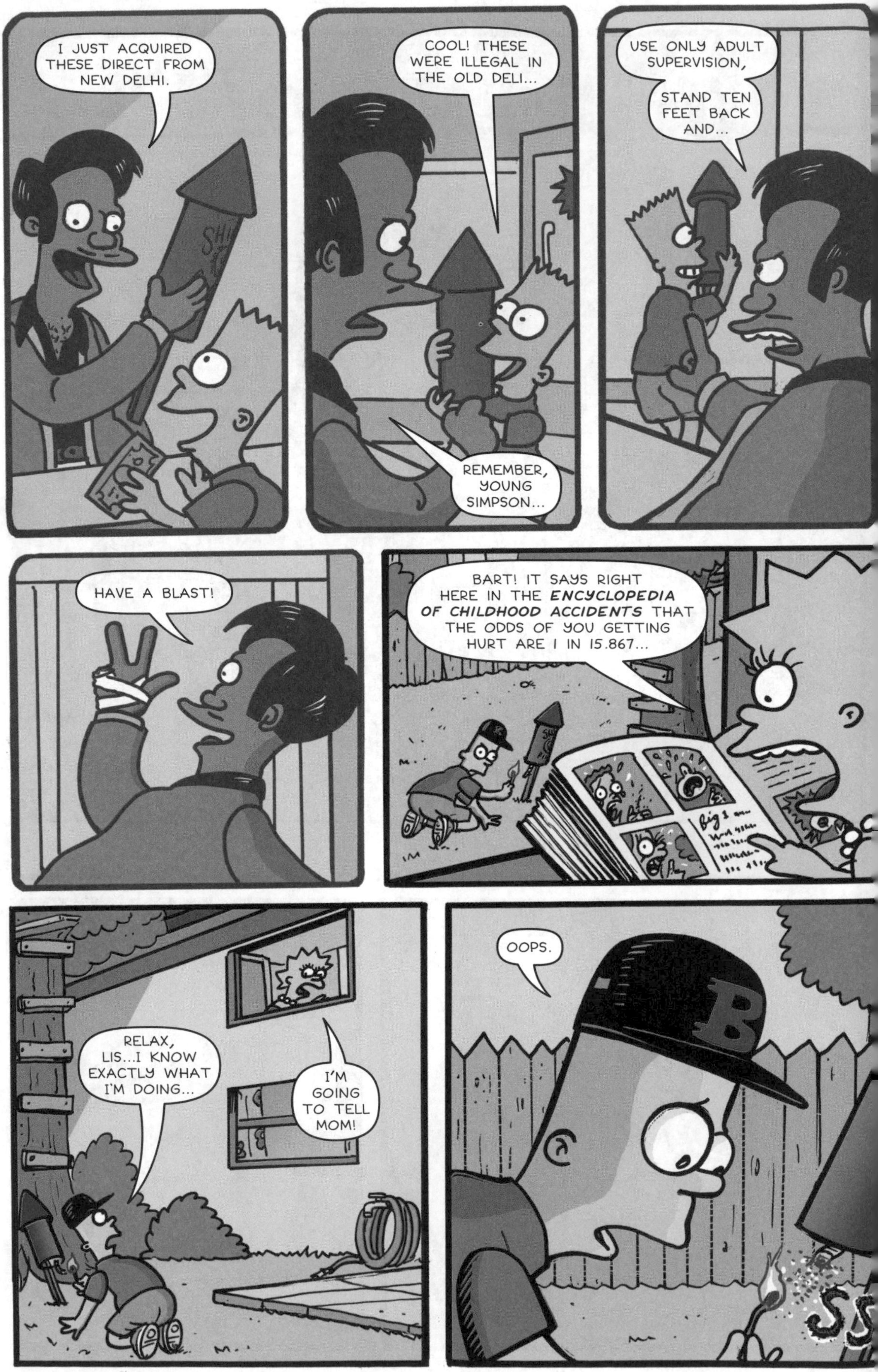
I JUST ACQUIRED THESE DIRECT FROM NEW DELHI.
COOL! THESE WERE ILLEGAL IN THE OLD DELI...
REMEMBER, YOUNG SIMPSON...
USE ONLY ADULT SUPERVISION,
STAND TEN FEET BACK AND...
HAVE A BLAST!
BART! IT SAYS RIGHT HERE IN THE ENCYCLOPEDIA OF CHILDHOOD ACCIDENTS THAT THE ODDS OF YOU GETTING HURT ARE 1 IN 15.867...
RELAX, LIS...I KNOW EXACTLY WHAT I'M DOING...
I'M GOING TO TELL MOM!
OOPS.

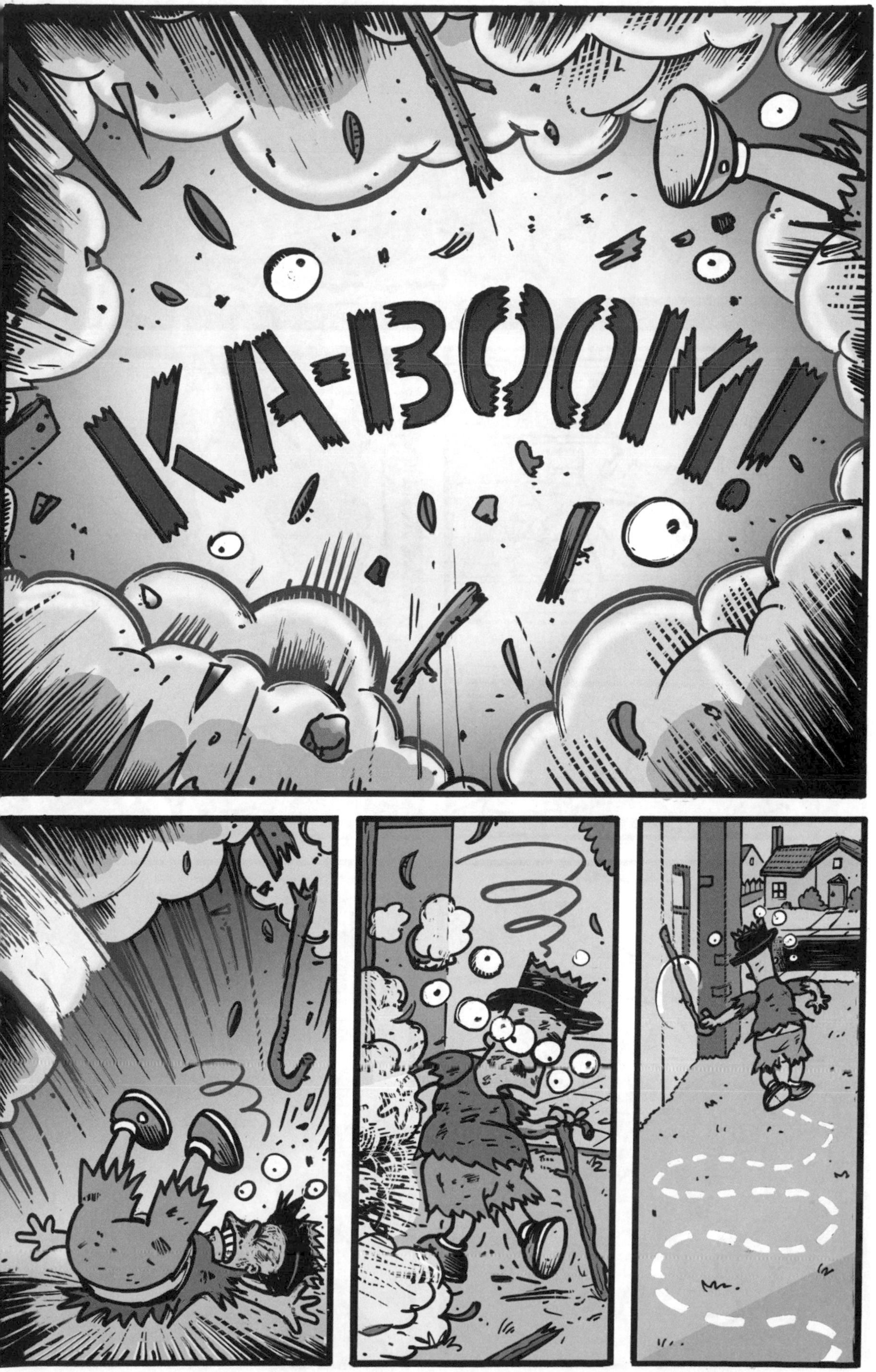
KA-BOOM!!

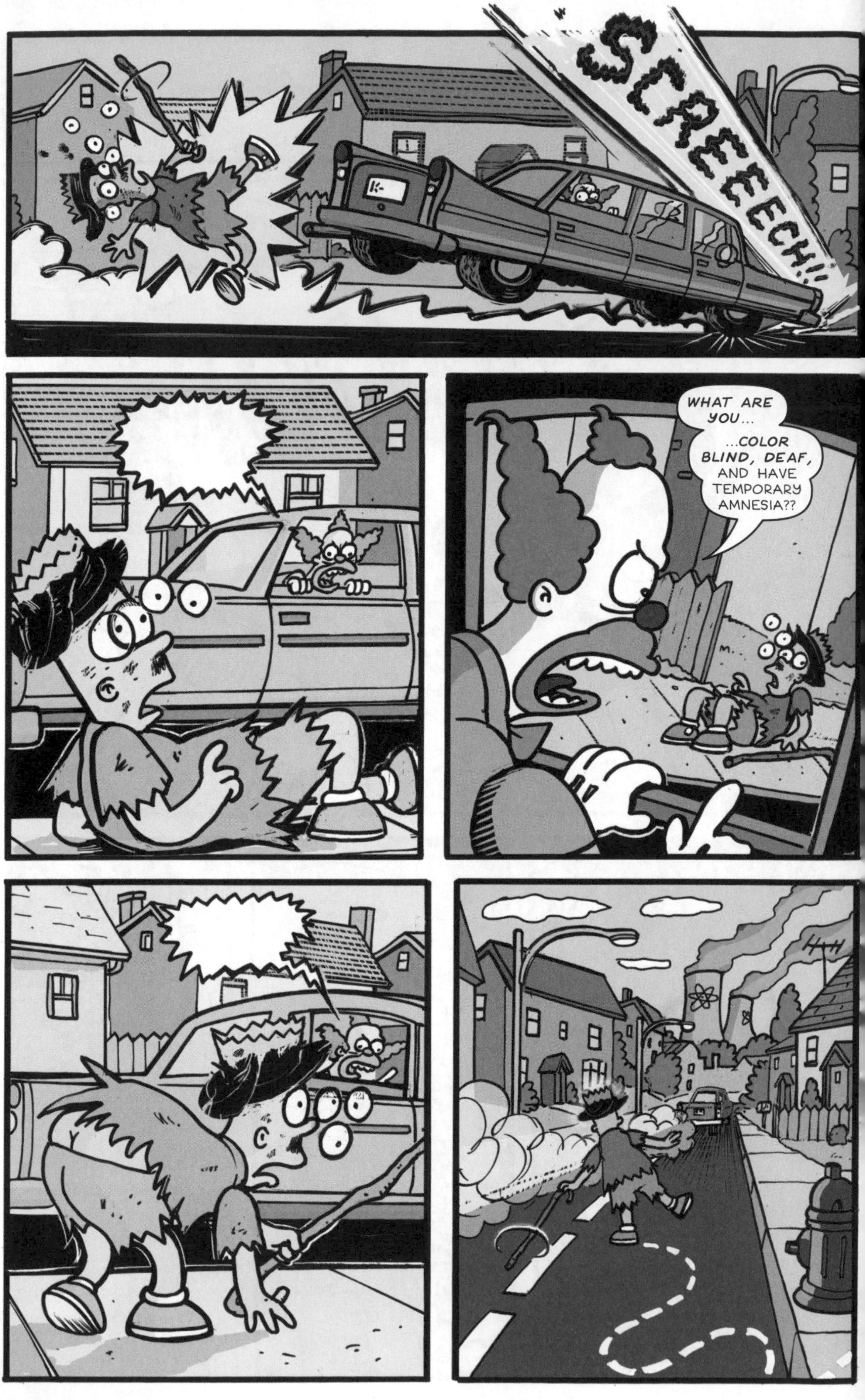
SCREEECH!!!
WHAT ARE YOU...
...COLOR BLIND, DEAF, AND HAVE TEMPORARY AMNESIA??

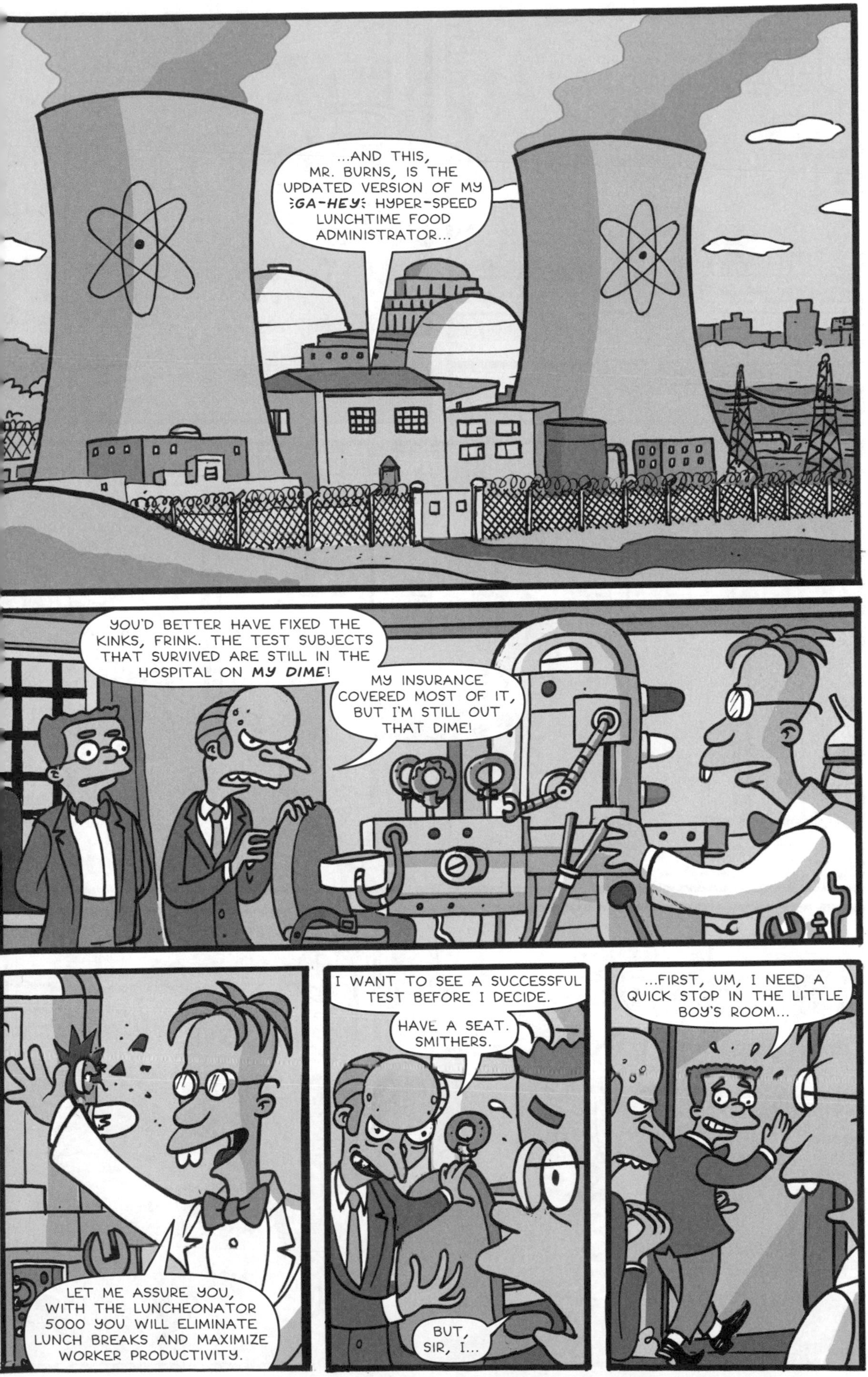
...AND THIS, MR. BURNS, IS THE UPDATED VERSION OF MY GA-HEY HYPER-SPEED LUNCHTIME FOOD ADMINISTRATOR...
YOU'D BETTER HAVE FIXED THE KINKS, FRINK. THE TEST SUBJECTS THAT SURVIVED ARE STILL IN THE HOSPITAL ON MY DIME!
MY INSURANCE COVERED MOST OF IT, BUT I'M STILL OUT THAT DIME!
LET ME ASSURE YOU, WITH THE LUNCHEONATOR 5000 YOU WILL ELIMINATE LUNCH BREAKS AND MAXIMIZE WORKER PRODUCTIVITY.
I WANT TO SEE A SUCCESSFUL TEST BEFORE I DECIDE.
HAVE A SEAT. SMITHERS.
BUT, SIR, I...
...FIRST, UM, I NEED A QUICK STOP IN THE LITTLE BOY'S ROOM...

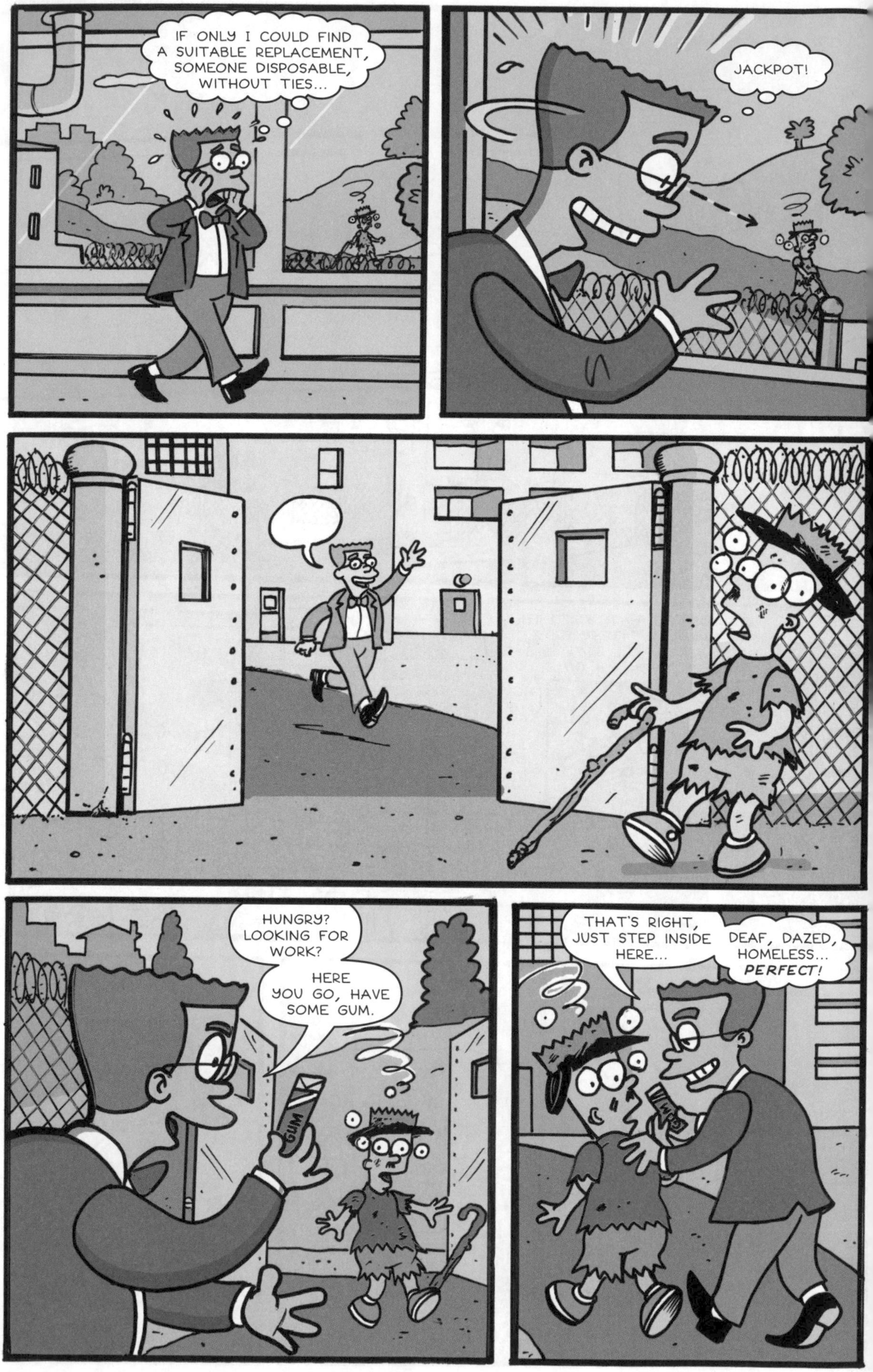
IF ONLY I COULD FIND A SUITABLE REPLACEMENT, SOMEONE DISPOSABLE, WITHOUT TIES...
JACKPOT!
HUNGRY? LOOKING FOR WORK?
HERE YOU GO, HAVE SOME GUM.
GUM
THAT'S RIGHT, JUST STEP INSIDE HERE...
DEAF, DAZED, HOMELESS... *PERFECT*!

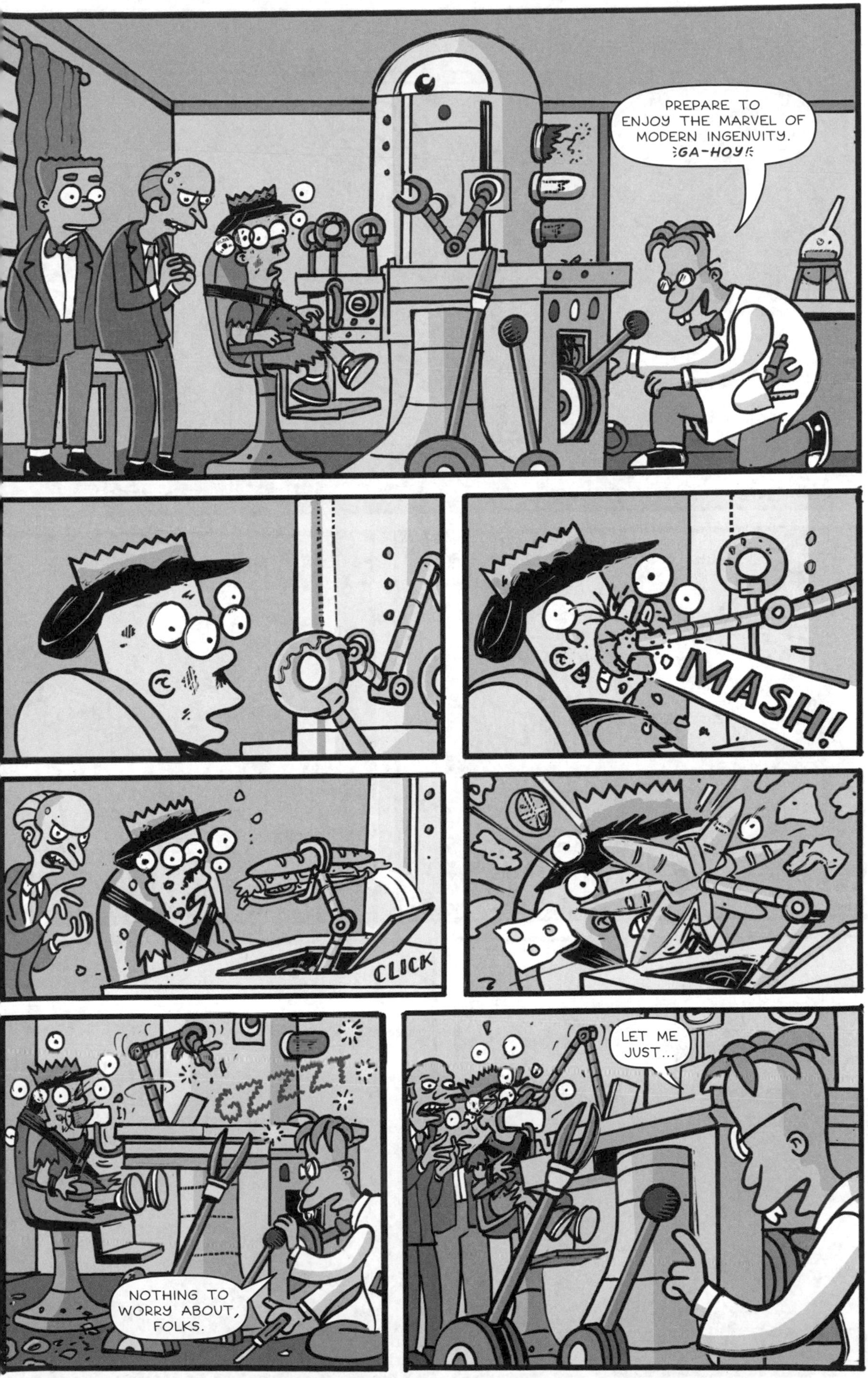
PREPARE TO ENJOY THE MARVEL OF MODERN INGENUITY. GA-HOY!
MASH!
CLICK
GZZZT
NOTHING TO WORRY ABOUT, FOLKS.
LET ME JUST...

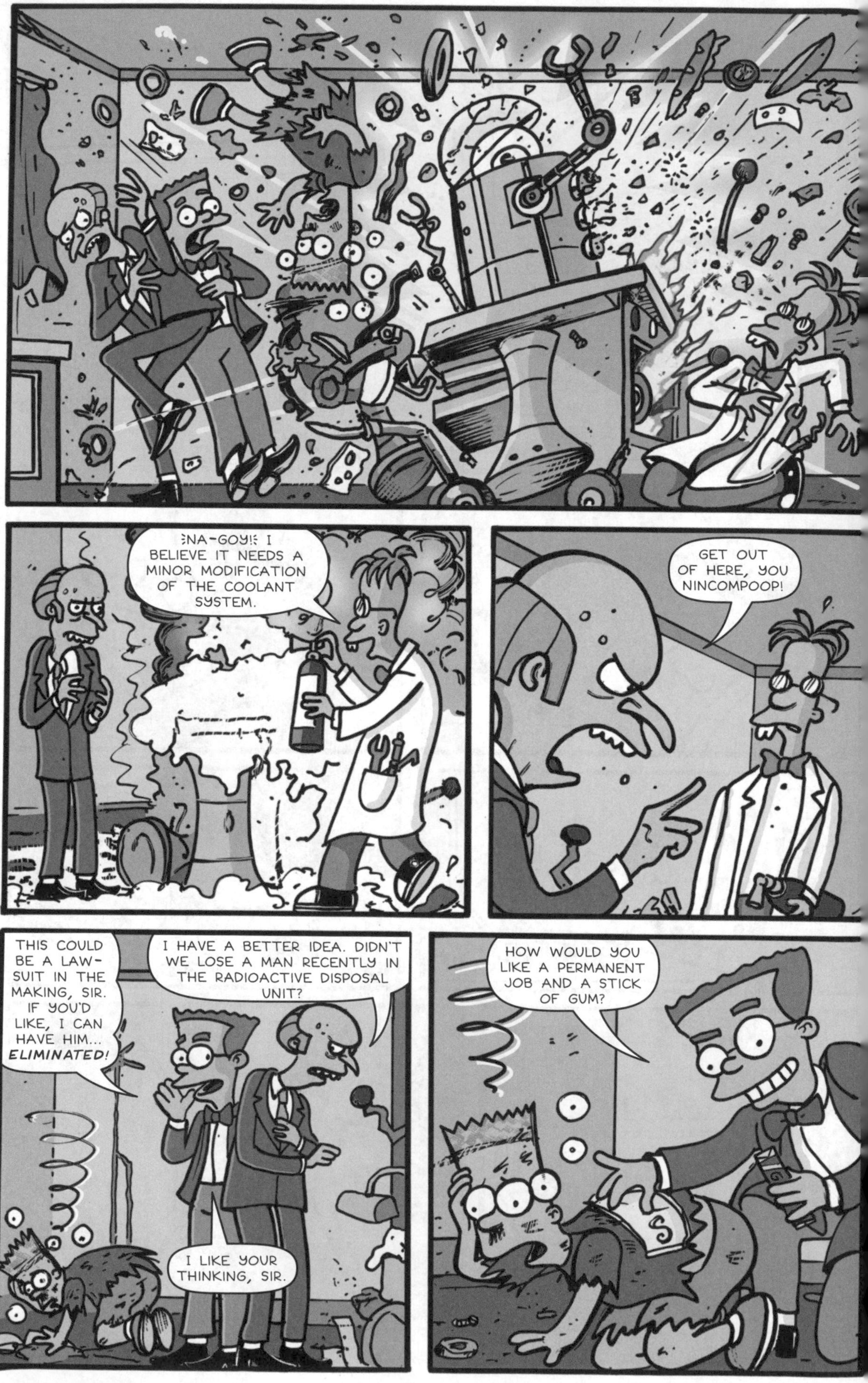

NA-GOY! I BELIEVE IT NEEDS A MINOR MODIFICATION OF THE COOLANT SYSTEM.
GET OUT OF HERE, YOU NINCOMPOOP!
THIS COULD BE A LAW-SUIT IN THE MAKING, SIR. IF YOU'D LIKE, I CAN HAVE HIM... *ELIMINATED!*
I HAVE A BETTER IDEA. DIDN'T WE LOSE A MAN RECENTLY IN THE RADIOACTIVE DISPOSAL UNIT?
I LIKE YOUR THINKING, SIR.
HOW WOULD YOU LIKE A PERMANENT JOB AND A STICK OF GUM?

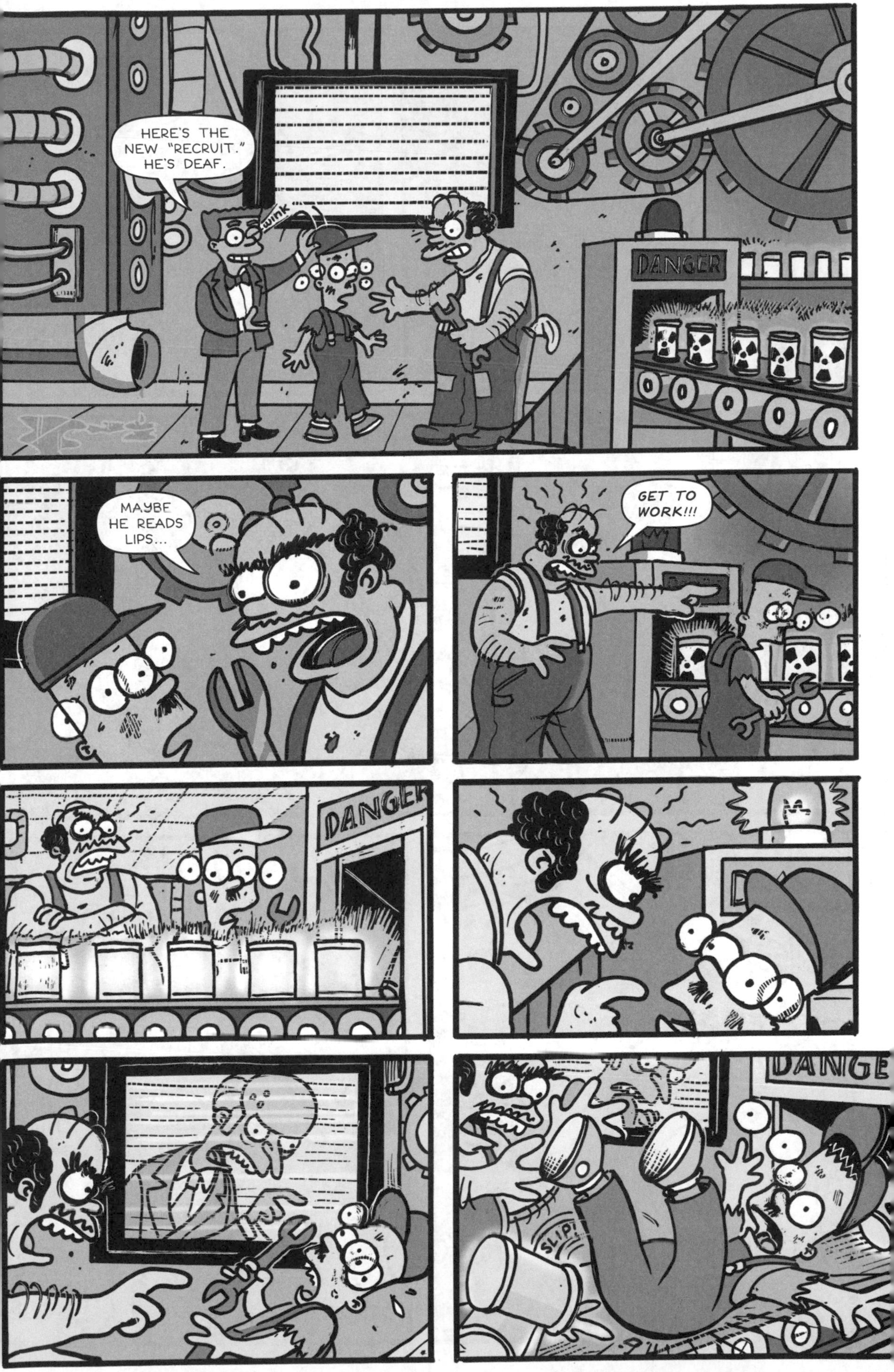
HERE'S THE NEW "RECRUIT." HE'S DEAF.
WINK
DANGER
MAYBE HE READS LIPS...
GET TO WORK!!!
DANGER
DANGE
SLIP!

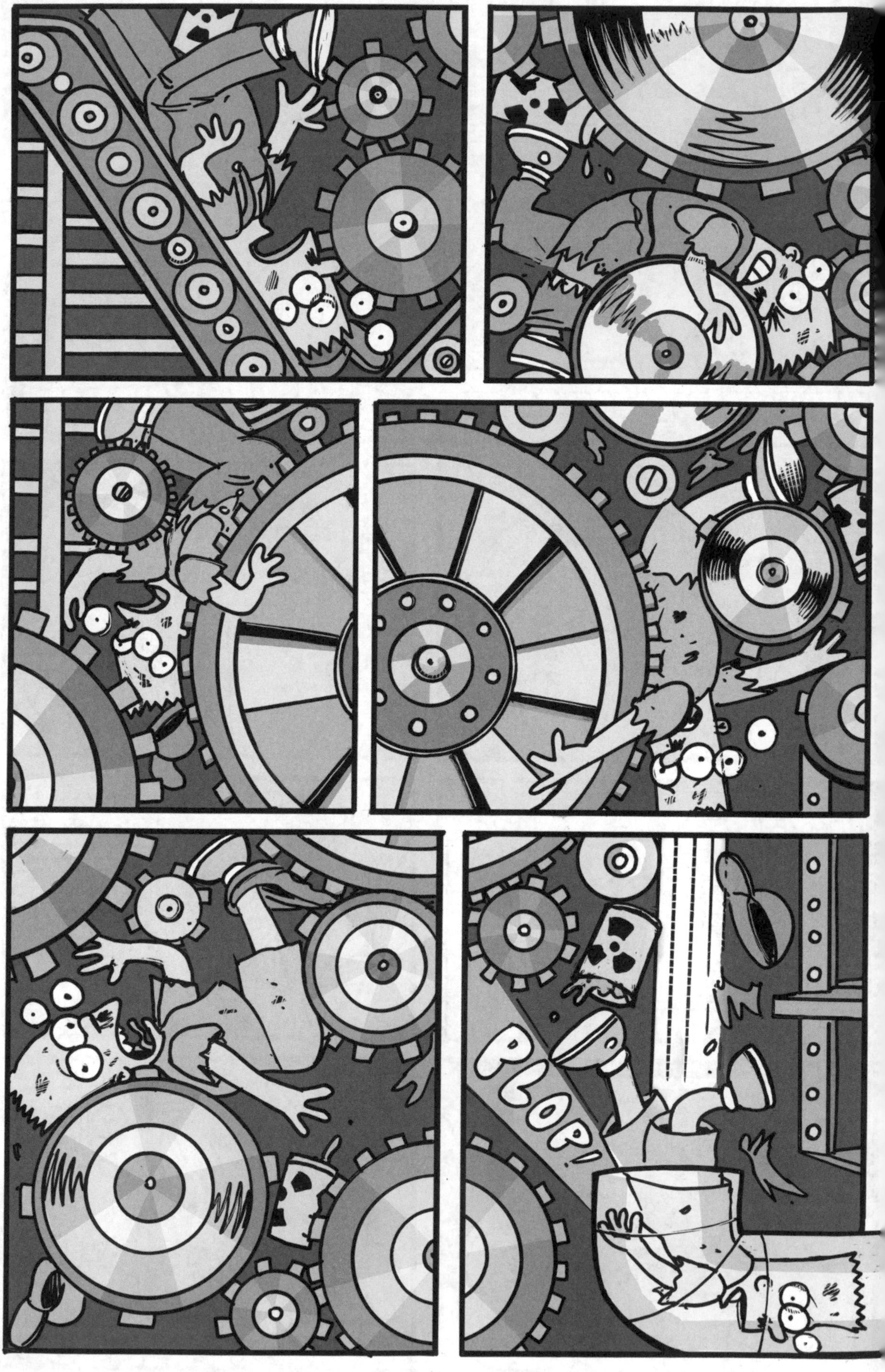
PLOP!

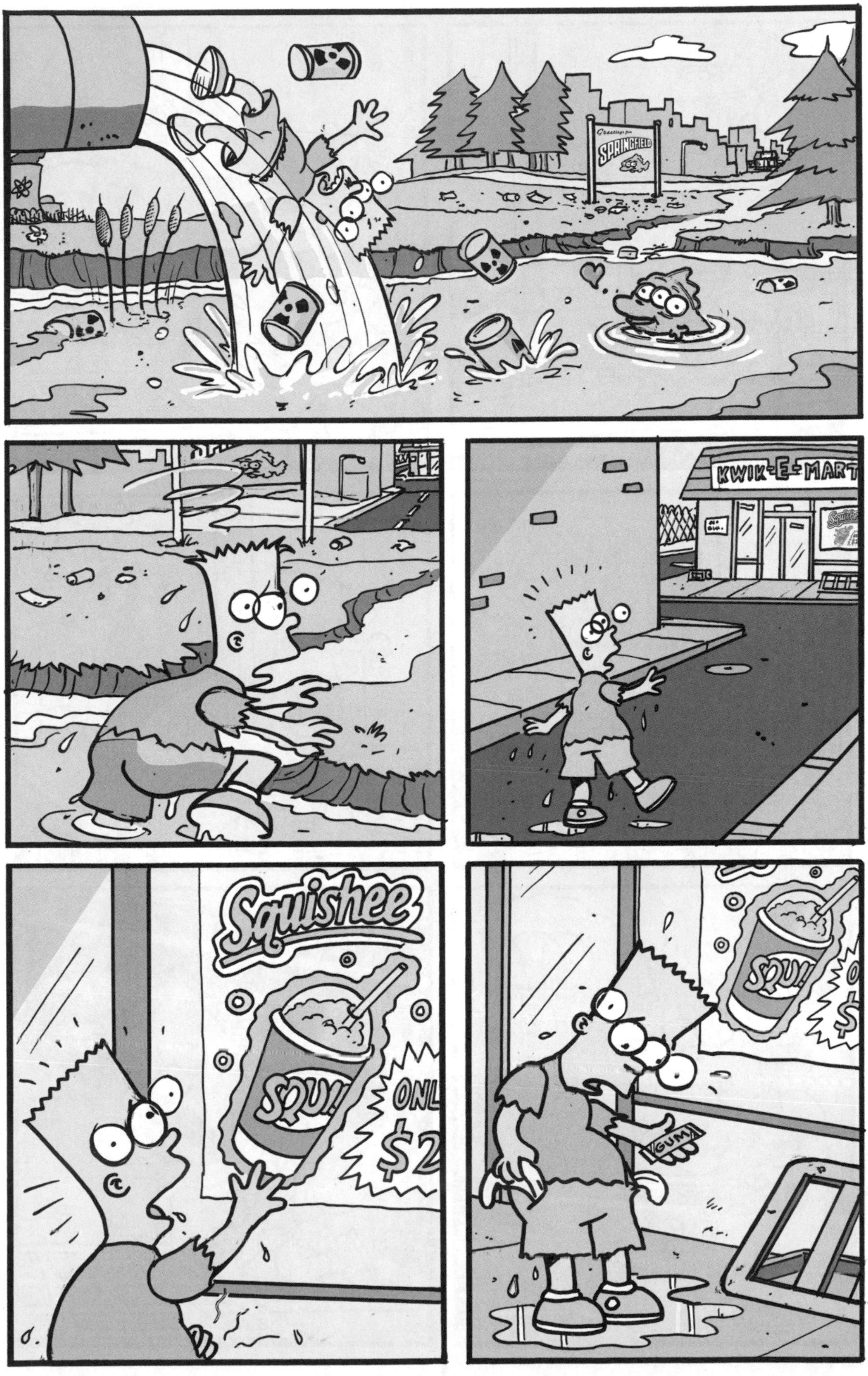
SPRINGFIELD
KWIK-E-MART
Squishee
SQU!
ONL
$2
GUM

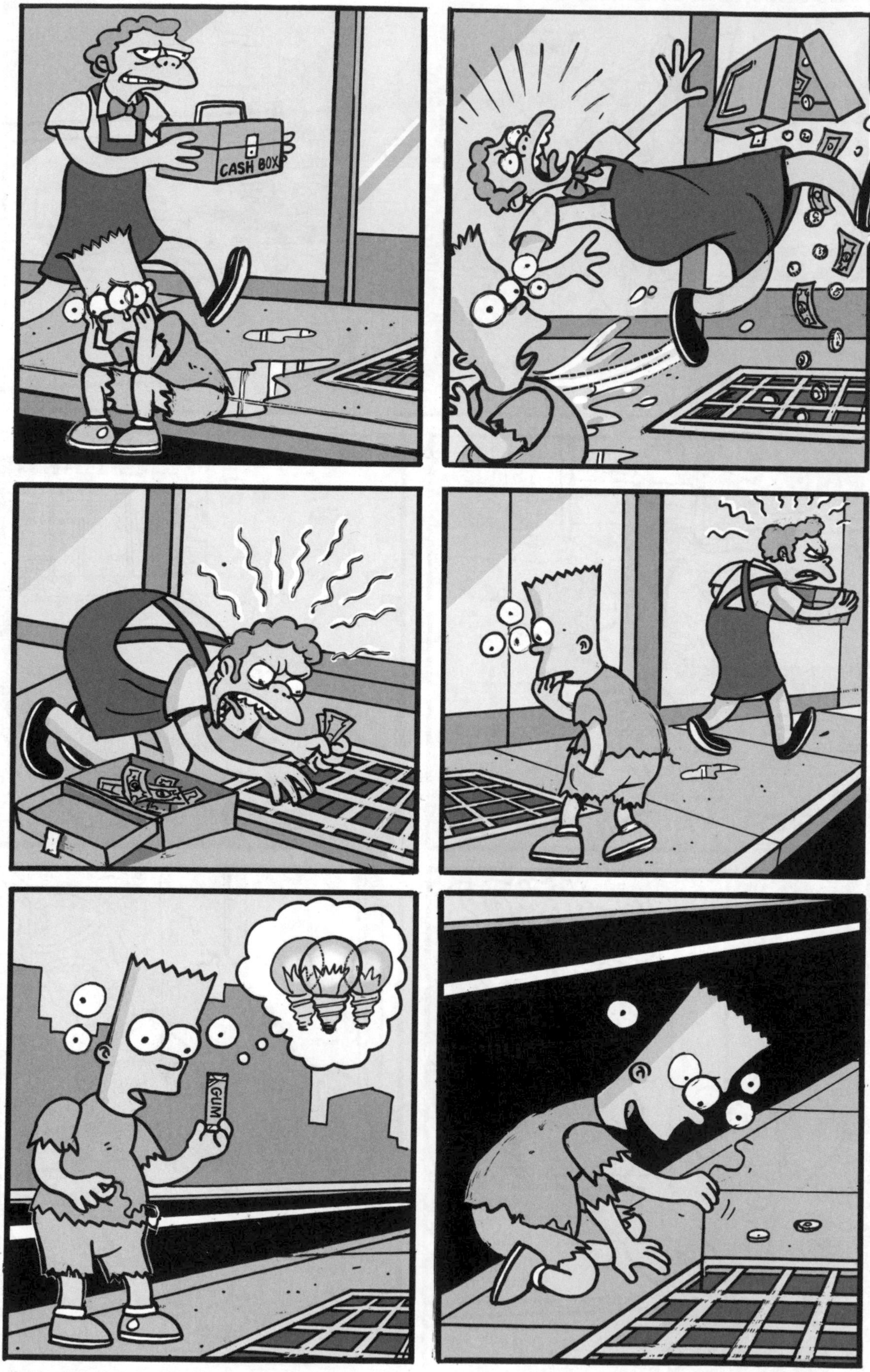
CASH BOX
GUM

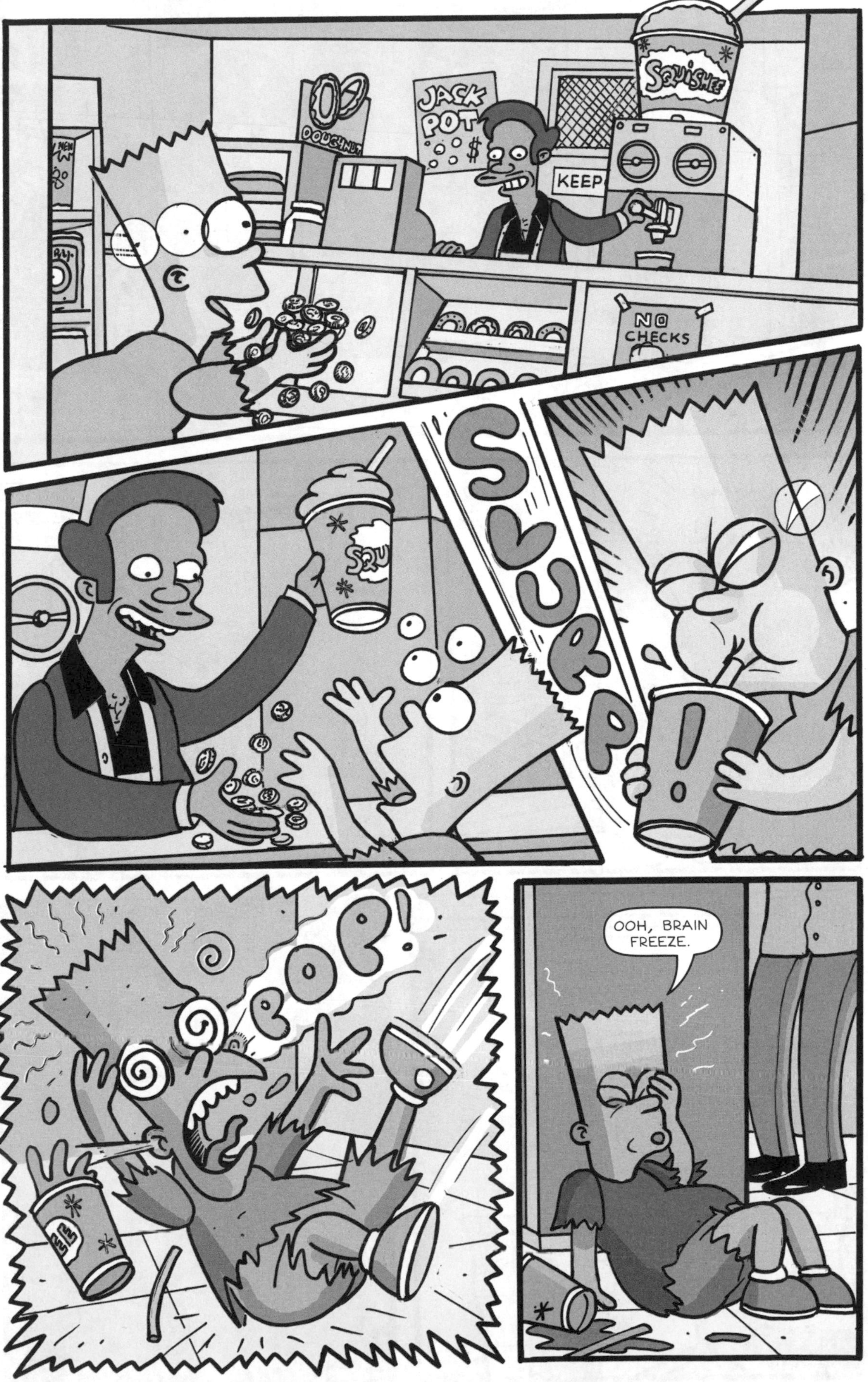
JACK POT
SQUISHEE
KEEP
NO CHECKS
SLURP!
POP!
OOH, BRAIN FREEZE.

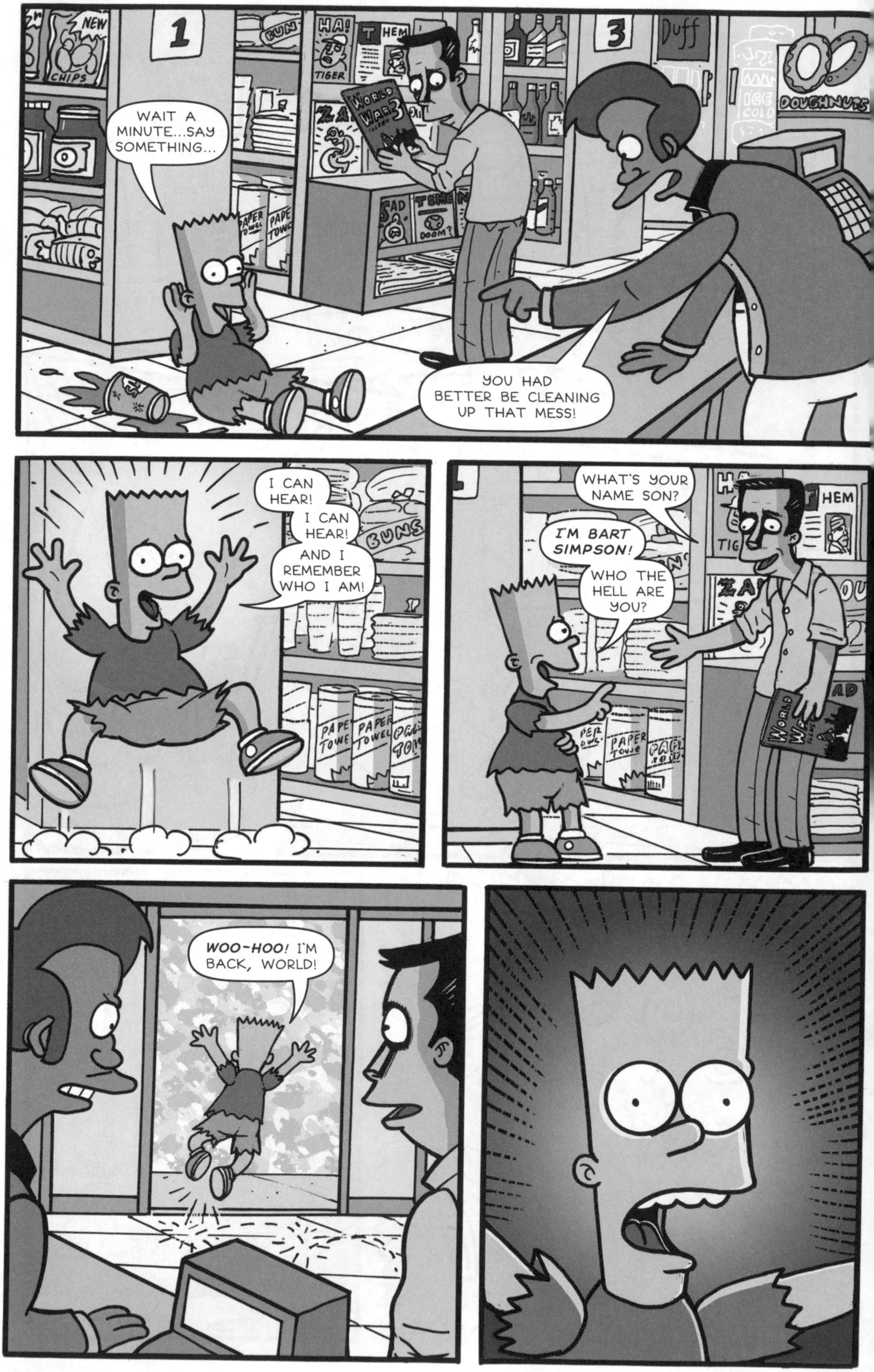
WAIT A MINUTE...SAY SOMETHING...
YOU HAD BETTER BE CLEANING UP THAT MESS!
I CAN HEAR!
I CAN HEAR!
AND I REMEMBER WHO I AM!
WHAT'S YOUR NAME SON?
I'M BART SIMPSON!
WHO THE HELL ARE YOU?
WOO-HOO! I'M BACK, WORLD!

THERE YOU GO, GUYS. ENJOY THE GAME.

NEW RELEASES
KING OF VIOLENCE 9
"OCEANS OF PAIN"
VAMPIRE SLEEP-OVER 3
GUN CRAZY 5
BUTTON MASHER 2
SOME DUMB PUPPY GAME

YOU KNOW IT!

BART SIMPSON IN

LET THE GAMES BEGIN!

OH BOY OH BOY OH BOY! *ENDLESS QUEST 2*! IT'S FINALLY *OURS*!

BEST $39.95 WE EVER SPENT EVER!

C'MON, MILHOUSE, LET'S GET BACK TO MY HOUSE AND POP THIS BAD BOY IN!

I THINK I'M GONNA FAINT I'M SO EXCITED! I CAN'T WAIT TO ENDLESSLY QUEST!

MATT GROENING

SOON...

C'MON, BART! HURRY UP! I WANNA PLAY!

I'M *TRYING*, MILHOUSE! ⦃UF!⦄ STUPID PLASTIC SEAL WON'T COME OFF!

CRINKLE CRINK

THE PLASTIC'S ALWAYS HARD TO GET OFF. TRY USING SCISSORS!

YOU WANT ME TO TRY?

DUH! I AM!

SCRRAADE

WAIT UP, I THINK I GOT IT! *WHOOPS!*

TEN MINUTES LATER...

BART! STOP SCRATCHING UP THE CASE!

WOULD YOU ⦃URRF⦄ SHUT UP, ALREADY! *AAARGGH!* THIS IS *RIDICULOUS!* STUPID SECURITY TAPE! WHY'S IT GOTTA BE SO STINKIN' *SECURE*?!

PICK PICK PICK

SKRITCH

EVAN DORKIN
STORY & ART

SARAH DYER
COLORS

KAREN BATES
LETTERS

BILL MORRISON
EDITOR

ANOTHER TWENTY MINUTES LATER...

I DON'T THINK THIS IS A GOOD IDEA, BART...

YOU WANNA PLAY ENDLESS QUEST BEFORE YOUR SEVENTIETH BIRTH-DAY? JUST HOLD STEADY AND DON'T SWEAT IT.

AND A ONE, AND A TWO AND A...

THREE...

...EEEOW!

OOF!

SP-CRACK

YOU B-BROKE THE CASE!

SO WHAT? IT'S OPEN, AIN'T IT?! ;PUFF; NOW ;HUFF; TO GET THE *DISC* OUT AND THEN...ETERNAL QUEST 2!

ANOTHER HALF HOUR LATER...

WHAT IS *WRONG* WITH THESE *STUPID GAME PEOPLE*?! ARE THEY *INSANE* MAKING THESE THINGS SO YOU CAN'T *OPEN* THEM?! *WHY DO THEY HATE AMERICA*?!

STUPID DISC! COME OUT, YOU STUPID DISC, OR I'LL KILL YOU!

BART, LET *ME* DO IT!

YOU'LL BREAK IT!

GO AWAY! GO AWAY, Y'HEAR ME? I GOT IT!

STUPID DISC! COME ON COME ON--!

SNAP!

?

?

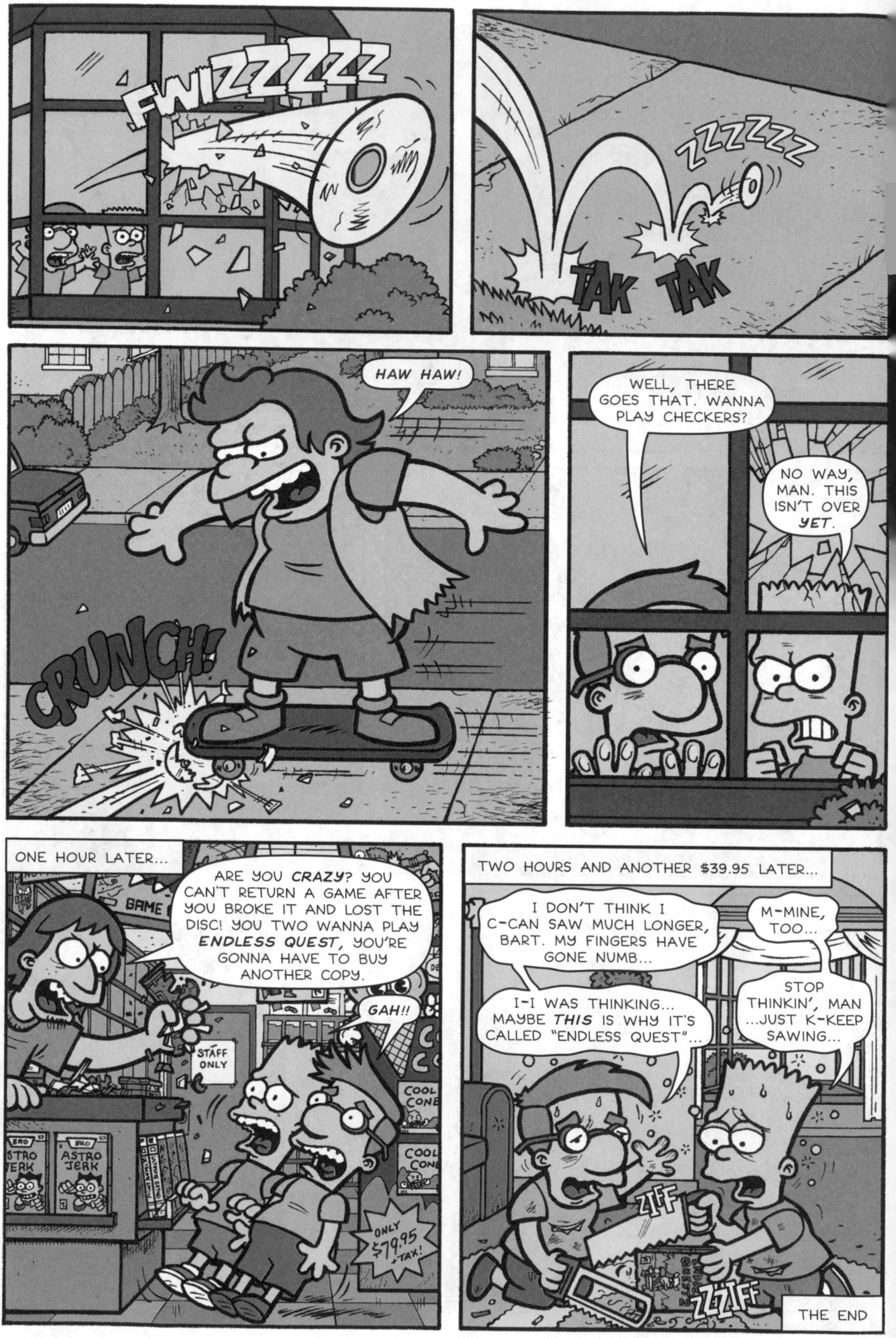
FWIZZZZZZ
ZZZZZZ
TAK TAK
HAW HAW!
CRUNCH!
WELL, THERE GOES THAT. WANNA PLAY CHECKERS?
NO WAY, MAN. THIS ISN'T OVER *YET*.
ONE HOUR LATER...
ARE YOU *CRAZY*? YOU CAN'T RETURN A GAME AFTER YOU BROKE IT AND LOST THE DISC! YOU TWO WANNA PLAY **ENDLESS QUEST**, YOU'RE GONNA HAVE TO BUY ANOTHER COPY.
GAH!!
STAFF ONLY
COOL CONE
ASTRO JERK
ONLY $79.95 +TAX!
TWO HOURS AND ANOTHER $39.95 LATER...
I DON'T THINK I C-CAN SAW MUCH LONGER, BART. MY FINGERS HAVE GONE NUMB...
M-MINE, TOO...
I-I WAS THINKING... MAYBE *THIS* IS WHY IT'S CALLED "ENDLESS QUEST"...
STOP THINKIN', MAN ...JUST K-KEEP SAWING...
ZIFF
ZZZIFF
THE END

LISA ROCKS THE PARTY!

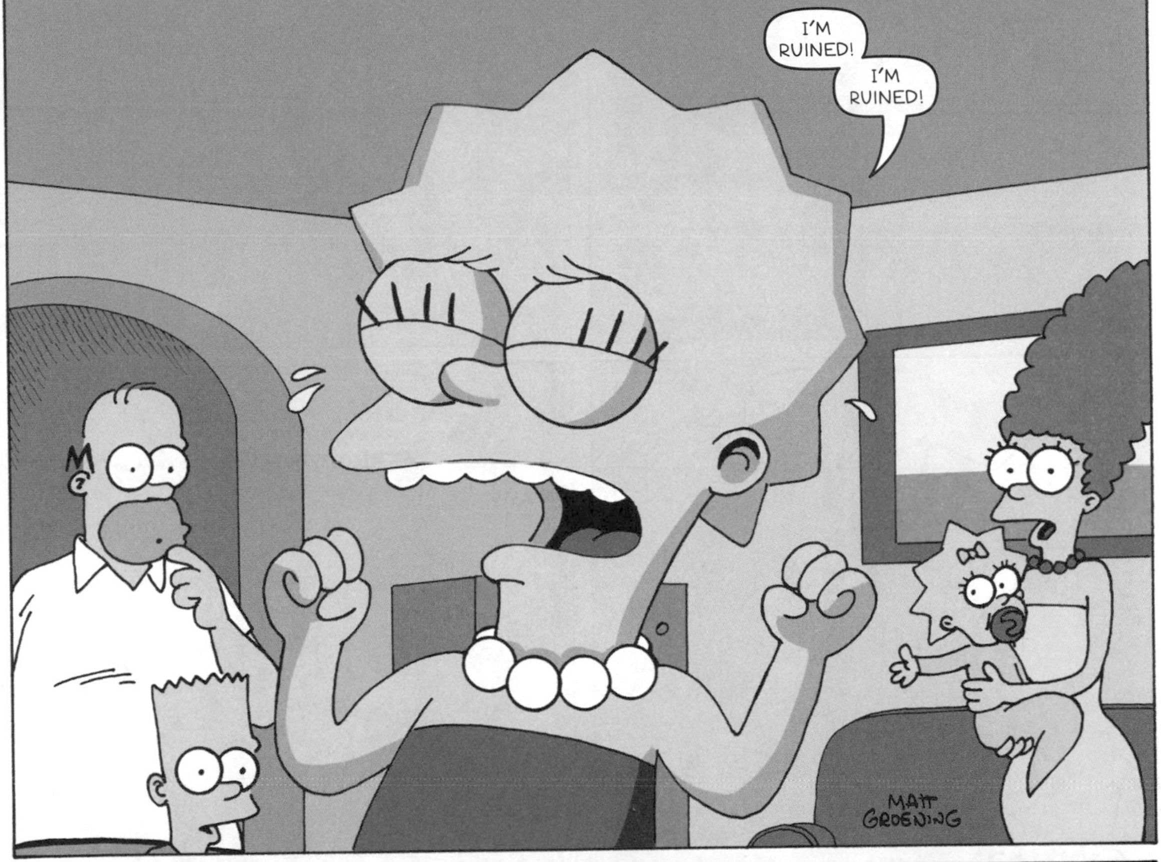
I'M RUINED! I'M RUINED!
MATT GROENING

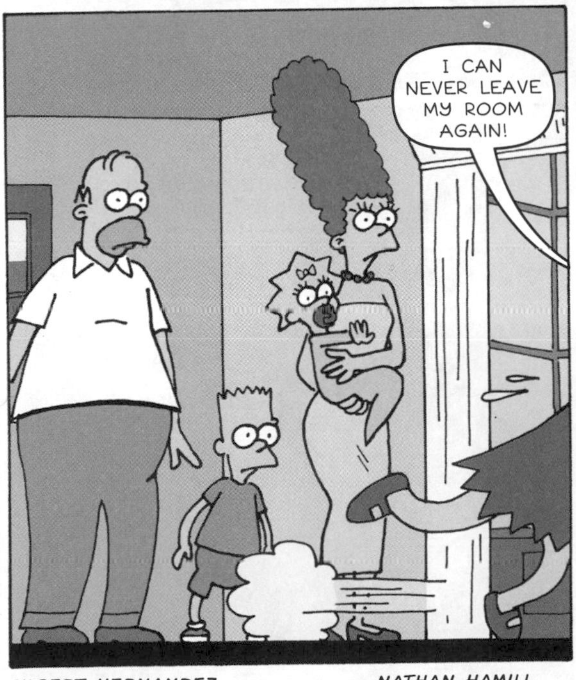
I CAN NEVER LEAVE MY ROOM AGAIN!

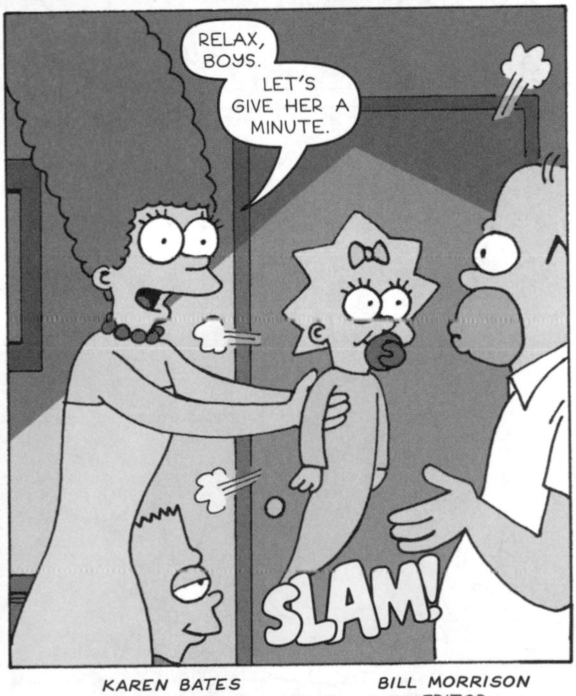
RELAX, BOYS. LET'S GIVE HER A MINUTE.
SLAM!

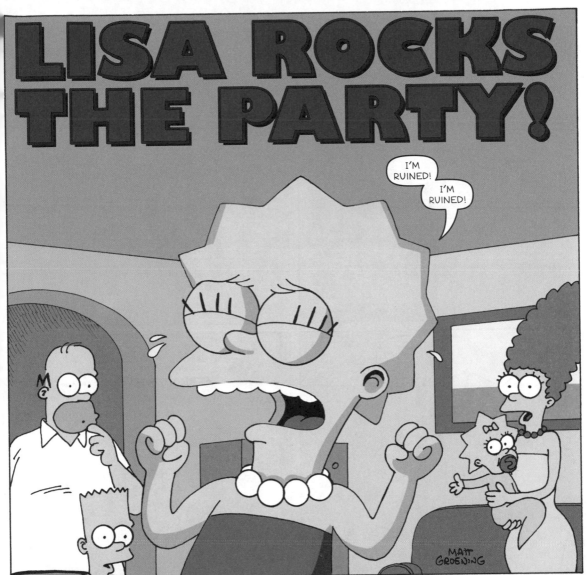

GILBERT HERNANDEZ
SCRIPT & ART

NATHAN HAMILL
COLORS

KAREN BATES
LETTERS

BILL MORRISON
EDITOR

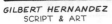

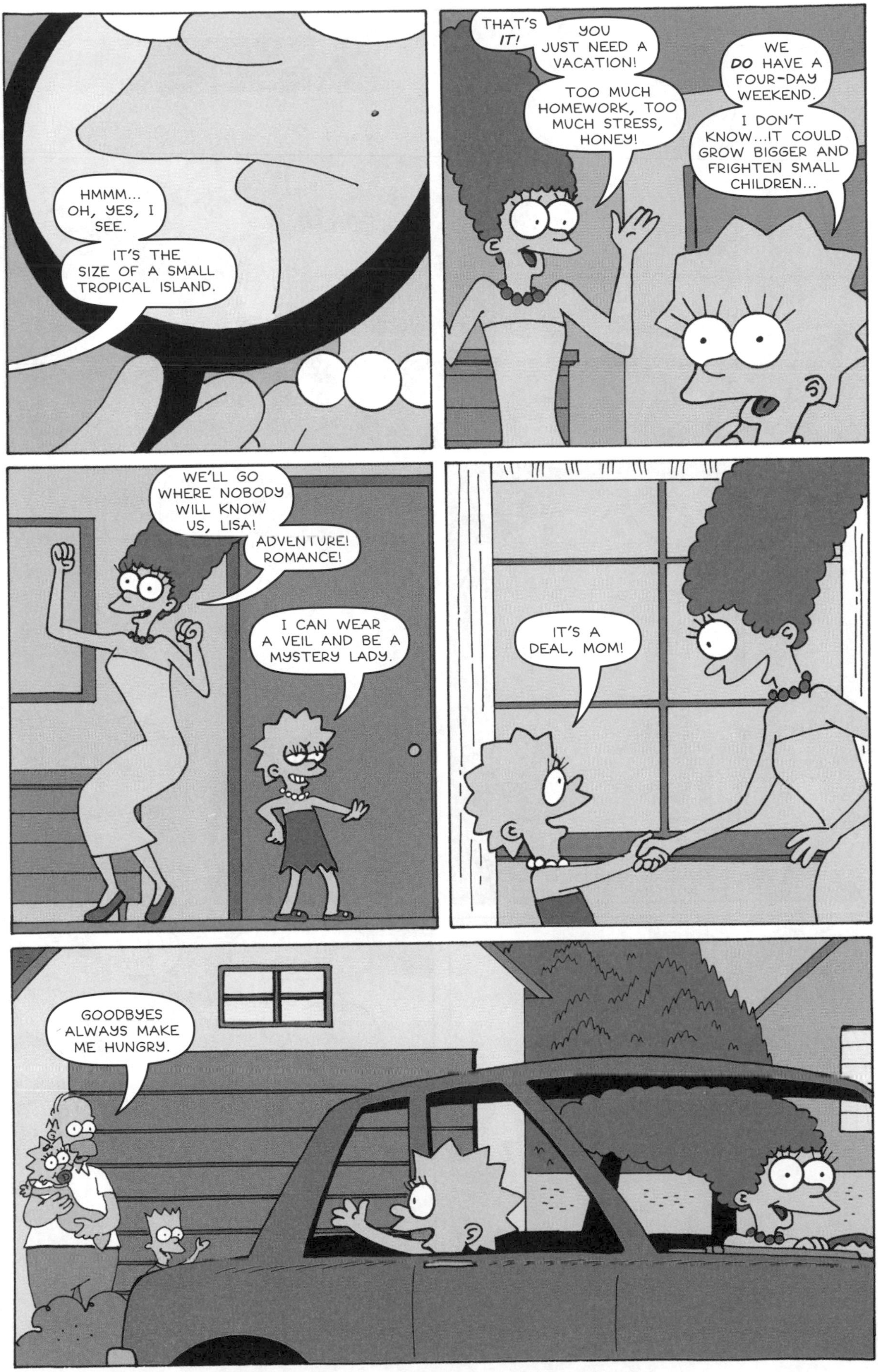
HMMM... OH, YES, I SEE.
IT'S THE SIZE OF A SMALL TROPICAL ISLAND.
THAT'S *IT*!
YOU JUST NEED A VACATION!
TOO MUCH HOMEWORK, TOO MUCH STRESS, HONEY!
WE **DO** HAVE A FOUR-DAY WEEKEND.
I DON'T KNOW...IT COULD GROW BIGGER AND FRIGHTEN SMALL CHILDREN...
WE'LL GO WHERE NOBODY WILL KNOW US, LISA!
ADVENTURE! ROMANCE!
I CAN WEAR A VEIL AND BE A MYSTERY LADY.
IT'S A DEAL, MOM!
GOODBYES ALWAYS MAKE ME HUNGRY.

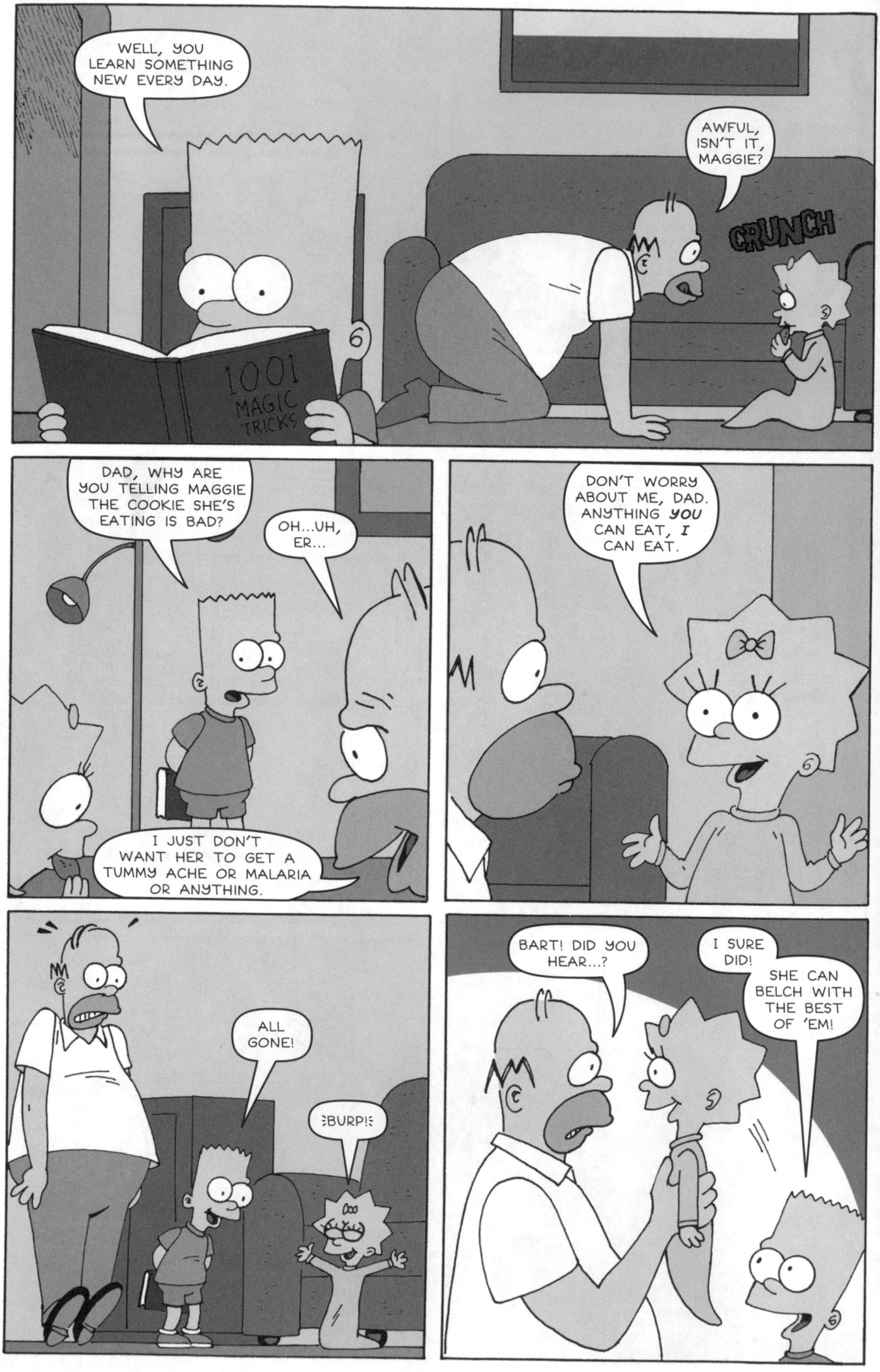
WELL, YOU LEARN SOMETHING NEW EVERY DAY.
1001 MAGIC TRICKS
AWFUL, ISN'T IT, MAGGIE?
CRUNCH
DAD, WHY ARE YOU TELLING MAGGIE THE COOKIE SHE'S EATING IS BAD?
OH...UH, ER...
I JUST DON'T WANT HER TO GET A TUMMY ACHE OR MALARIA OR ANYTHING.
DON'T WORRY ABOUT ME, DAD. ANYTHING *YOU* CAN EAT, *I* CAN EAT.
ALL GONE!
BURP!
BART! DID YOU HEAR...?
I SURE DID!
SHE CAN BELCH WITH THE BEST OF 'EM!

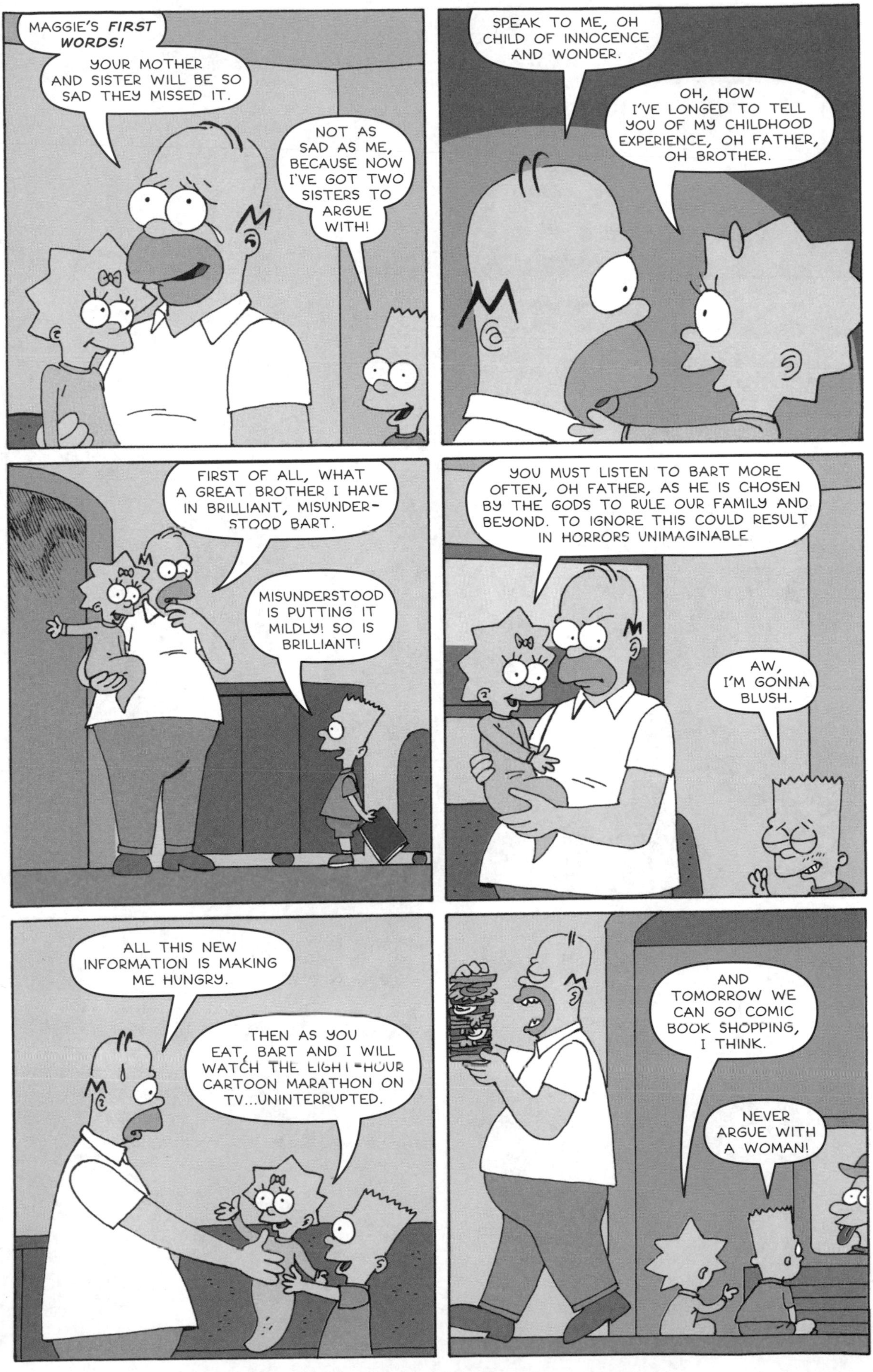
MAGGIE'S **FIRST WORDS!**
YOUR MOTHER AND SISTER WILL BE SO SAD THEY MISSED IT.
NOT AS SAD AS ME, BECAUSE NOW I'VE GOT TWO SISTERS TO ARGUE WITH!
SPEAK TO ME, OH CHILD OF INNOCENCE AND WONDER.
OH, HOW I'VE LONGED TO TELL YOU OF MY CHILDHOOD EXPERIENCE, OH FATHER, OH BROTHER.
FIRST OF ALL, WHAT A GREAT BROTHER I HAVE IN BRILLIANT, MISUNDER-STOOD BART.
MISUNDERSTOOD IS PUTTING IT MILDLY! SO IS BRILLIANT!
YOU MUST LISTEN TO BART MORE OFTEN, OH FATHER, AS HE IS CHOSEN BY THE GODS TO RULE OUR FAMILY AND BEYOND. TO IGNORE THIS COULD RESULT IN HORRORS UNIMAGINABLE.
AW, I'M GONNA BLUSH.
ALL THIS NEW INFORMATION IS MAKING ME HUNGRY.
THEN AS YOU EAT, BART AND I WILL WATCH THE EIGHT-HOUR CARTOON MARATHON ON TV...UNINTERRUPTED.
AND TOMORROW WE CAN GO COMIC BOOK SHOPPING, I THINK.
NEVER ARGUE WITH A WOMAN!

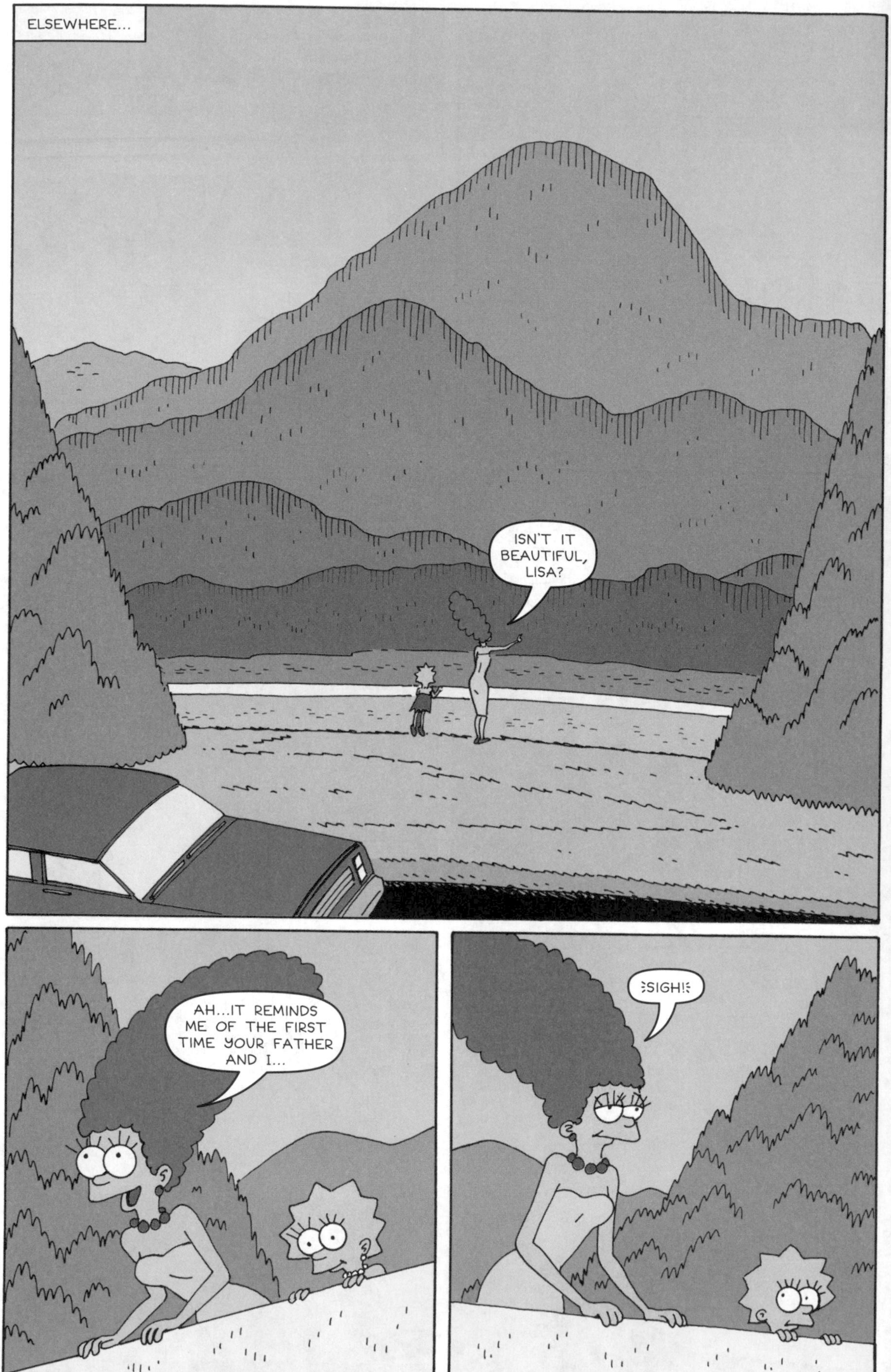
ELSEWHERE...
ISN'T IT BEAUTIFUL, LISA?
AH...IT REMINDS ME OF THE FIRST TIME YOUR FATHER AND I...
SIGH!

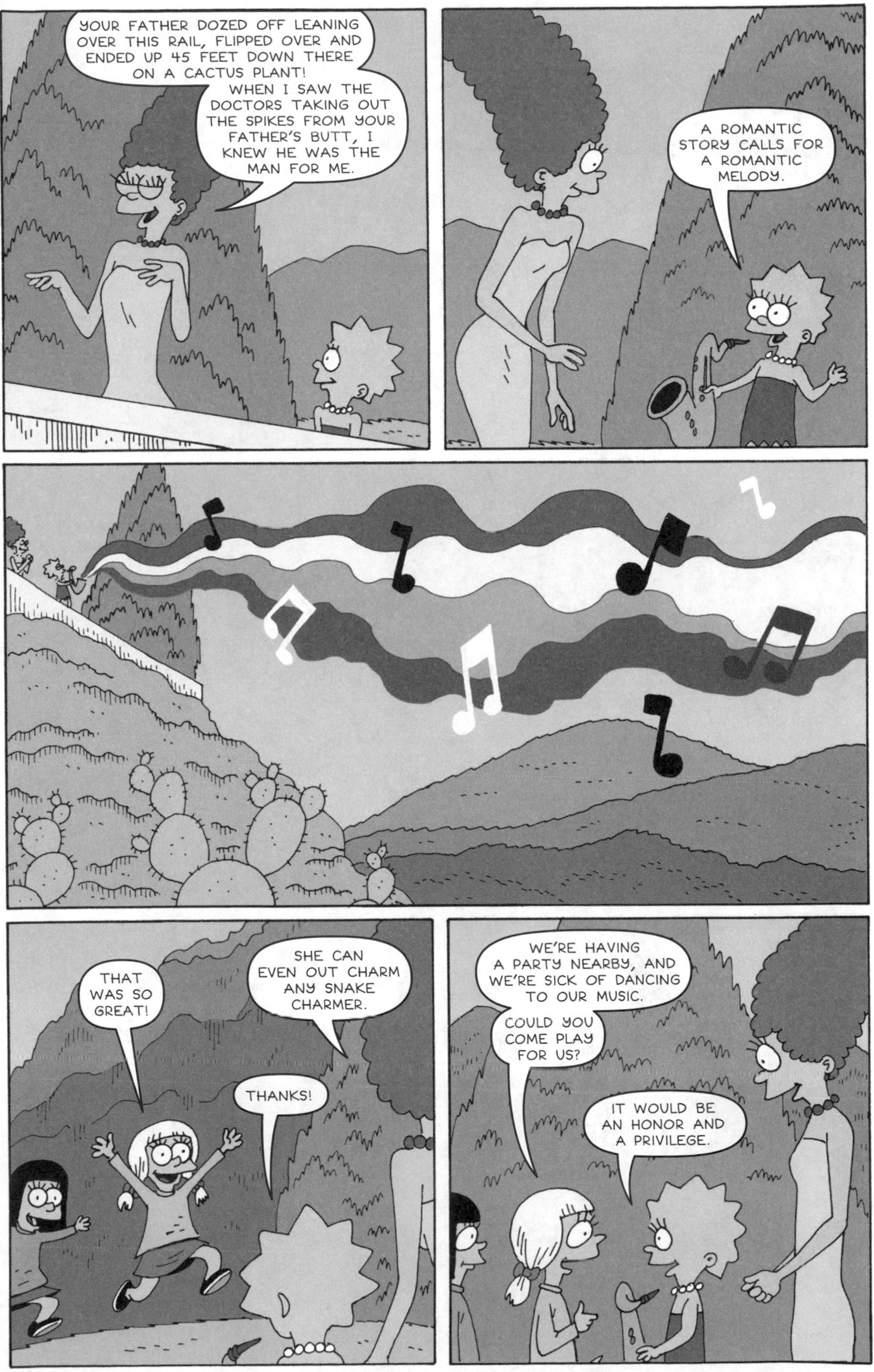

YOUR FATHER DOZED OFF LEANING OVER THIS RAIL, FLIPPED OVER AND ENDED UP 45 FEET DOWN THERE ON A CACTUS PLANT!
WHEN I SAW THE DOCTORS TAKING OUT THE SPIKES FROM YOUR FATHER'S BUTT, I KNEW HE WAS THE MAN FOR ME.
A ROMANTIC STORY CALLS FOR A ROMANTIC MELODY.
THAT WAS SO GREAT!
SHE CAN EVEN OUT CHARM ANY SNAKE CHARMER.
THANKS!
WE'RE HAVING A PARTY NEARBY, AND WE'RE SICK OF DANCING TO OUR MUSIC.
COULD YOU COME PLAY FOR US?
IT WOULD BE AN HONOR AND A PRIVILEGE.

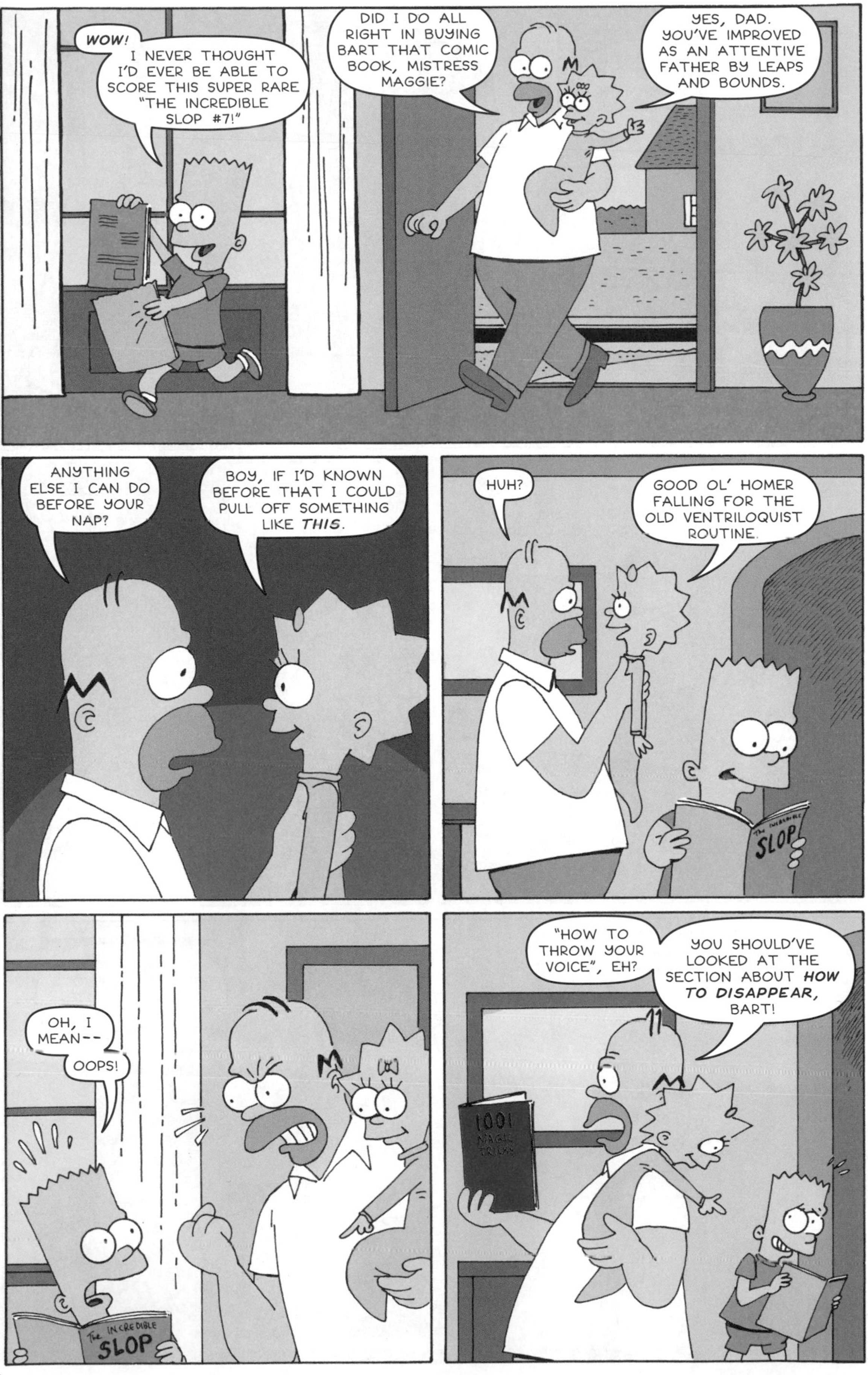
WOW! I NEVER THOUGHT I'D EVER BE ABLE TO SCORE THIS SUPER RARE "THE INCREDIBLE SLOP #7!"
DID I DO ALL RIGHT IN BUYING BART THAT COMIC BOOK, MISTRESS MAGGIE?
YES, DAD. YOU'VE IMPROVED AS AN ATTENTIVE FATHER BY LEAPS AND BOUNDS.
ANYTHING ELSE I CAN DO BEFORE YOUR NAP?
BOY, IF I'D KNOWN BEFORE THAT I COULD PULL OFF SOMETHING LIKE THIS.
HUH?
GOOD OL' HOMER FALLING FOR THE OLD VENTRILOQUIST ROUTINE.
The INCREDIBLE SLOP
OH, I MEAN--
OOPS!
The INCREDIBLE SLOP
"HOW TO THROW YOUR VOICE", EH?
YOU SHOULD'VE LOOKED AT THE SECTION ABOUT HOW TO DISAPPEAR, BART!
1001 MAGIC TRICKS

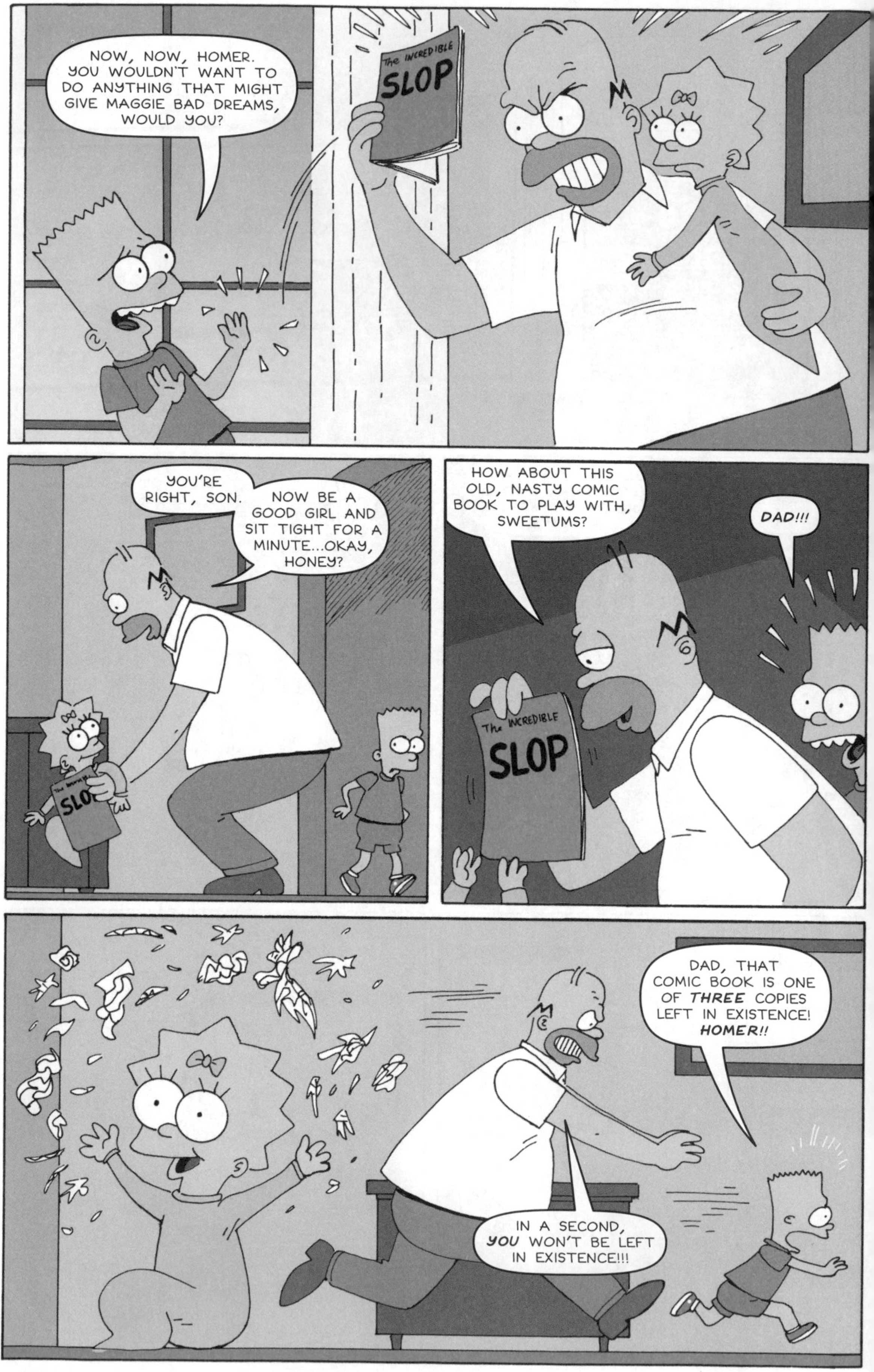
NOW, NOW, HOMER. YOU WOULDN'T WANT TO DO ANYTHING THAT MIGHT GIVE MAGGIE BAD DREAMS, WOULD YOU?
The INCREDIBLE SLOP
YOU'RE RIGHT, SON.
NOW BE A GOOD GIRL AND SIT TIGHT FOR A MINUTE...OKAY, HONEY?
HOW ABOUT THIS OLD, NASTY COMIC BOOK TO PLAY WITH, SWEETUMS?
DAD!!!
The INCREDIBLE SLOP
DAD, THAT COMIC BOOK IS ONE OF THREE COPIES LEFT IN EXISTENCE! HOMER!!
IN A SECOND, YOU WON'T BE LEFT IN EXISTENCE!!!

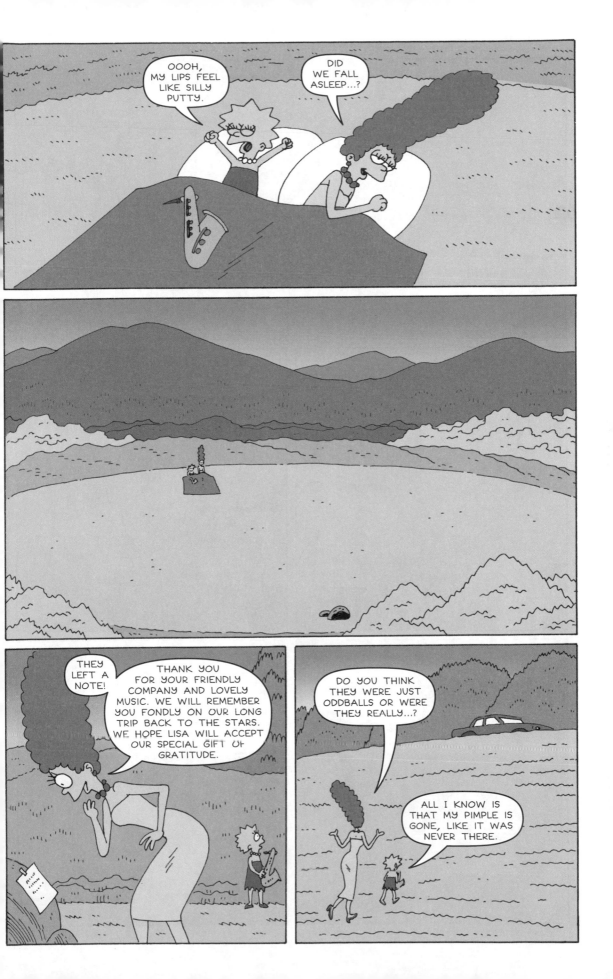

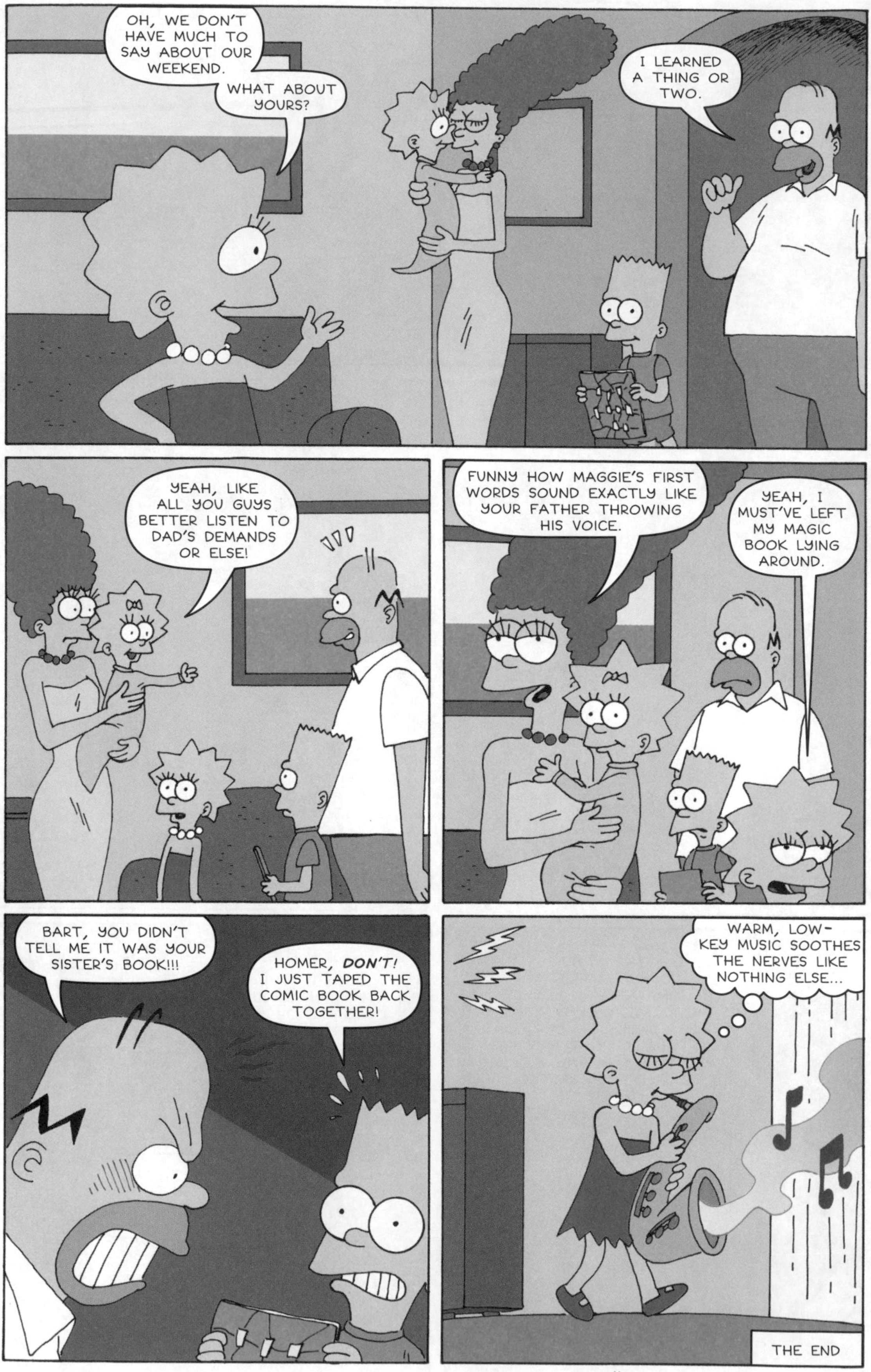

OH, WE DON'T HAVE MUCH TO SAY ABOUT OUR WEEKEND.
WHAT ABOUT YOURS?
I LEARNED A THING OR TWO.
YEAH, LIKE ALL YOU GUYS BETTER LISTEN TO DAD'S DEMANDS OR ELSE!
FUNNY HOW MAGGIE'S FIRST WORDS SOUND EXACTLY LIKE YOUR FATHER THROWING HIS VOICE.
YEAH, I MUST'VE LEFT MY MAGIC BOOK LYING AROUND.
BART, YOU DIDN'T TELL ME IT WAS YOUR SISTER'S BOOK!!!
HOMER, DON'T! I JUST TAPED THE COMIC BOOK BACK TOGETHER!
WARM, LOW-KEY MUSIC SOOTHES THE NERVES LIKE NOTHING ELSE...
THE END

MAGGIE'S CRIB

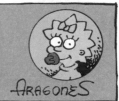

by ARAGONES

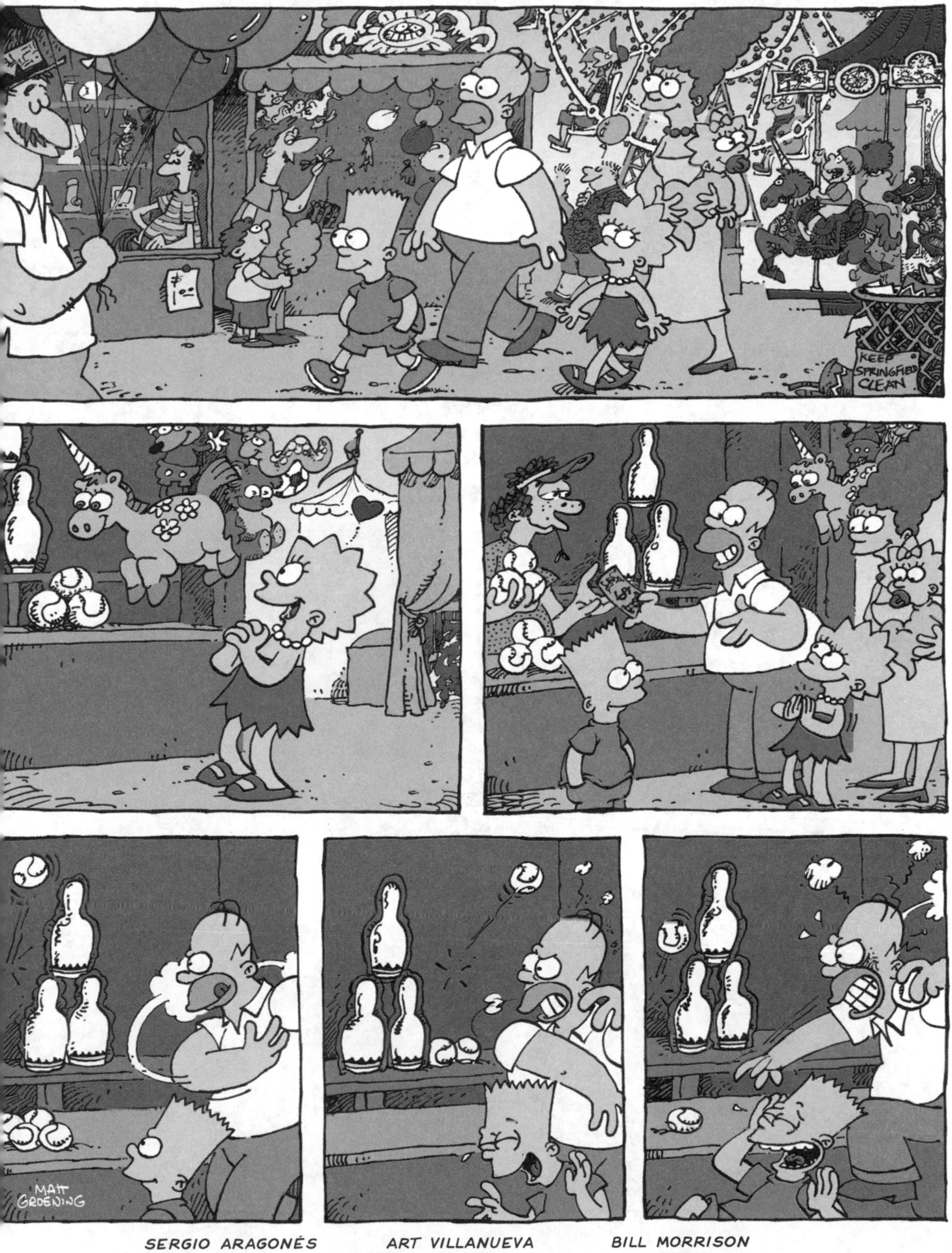
KEEP SPRINGFIELD CLEAN
MATT GROENING

SERGIO ARAGONÉS
STORY & ART

ART VILLANUEVA
COLORS

BILL MORRISON
EDITOR

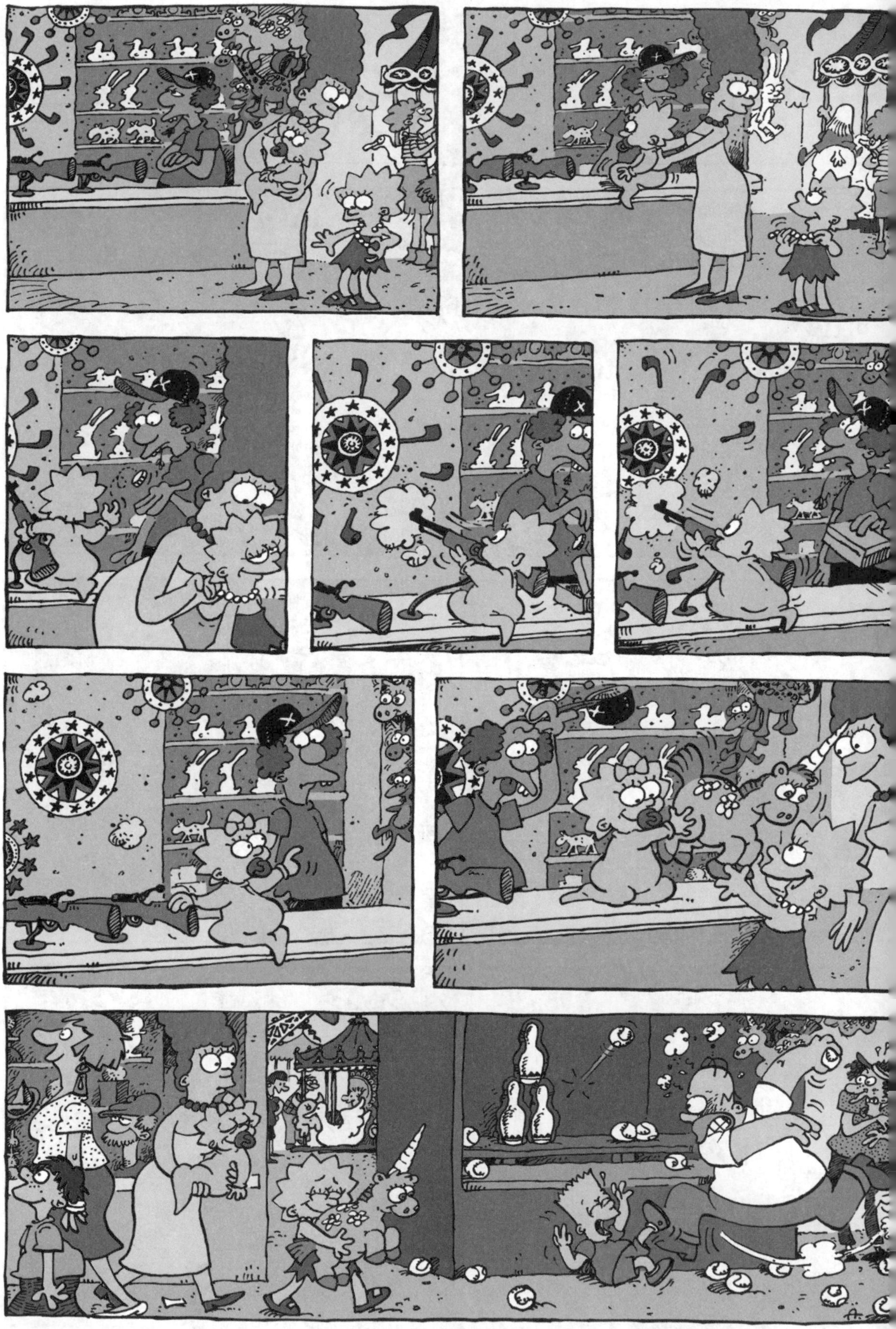

:YAWN!: TIME TO TACKLE ANOTHER DAY, JUST LIKE I TACKLED THE WRESTLING MONKEY IN MY SMASH HIT FILM, *TACKLE THAT MONKEY!*

♪ NINETY-NINE LUFTBALLOONS, AUF IHREM WEG ZUM HORIZONT... ♪

MATT GROENING

WHA--?!

ZOMBIE HAMLET

COMING SOON

THE NINJA WORE SNEAKERS

McBAIN THE MUSICAL!

NOOOOOO!!

McBAIN FOREVER

— JULY 26 —

THE DAY OF THE MUSTACHE

ARIE KAPLAN SCRIPT

NINA MATSUMOTO PENCILS

MIKE ROTE INKS

ART VILLANUEVA COLORS

KAREN BATES LETTERS

BILL MORRISON EDITOR

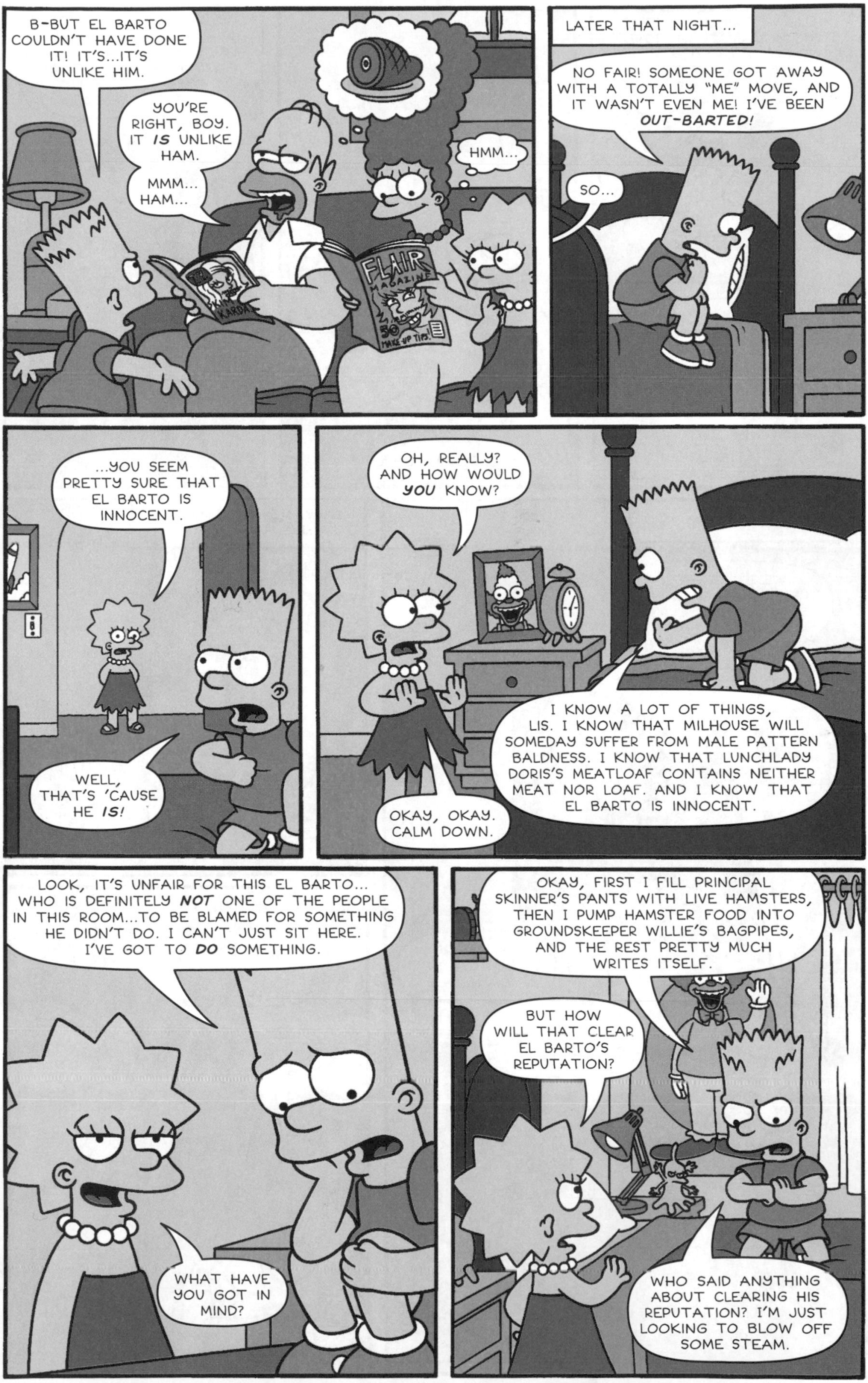
B-BUT EL BARTO COULDN'T HAVE DONE IT! IT'S...IT'S UNLIKE HIM.
YOU'RE RIGHT, BOY. IT *IS* UNLIKE HAM.
MMM... HAM...
HMM...
LATER THAT NIGHT...
NO FAIR! SOMEONE GOT AWAY WITH A TOTALLY "ME" MOVE, AND IT WASN'T EVEN ME! I'VE BEEN *OUT-BARTED!*
SO...
...YOU SEEM PRETTY SURE THAT EL BARTO IS INNOCENT.
WELL, THAT'S 'CAUSE HE *IS*!
OH, REALLY? AND HOW WOULD *YOU* KNOW?
I KNOW A LOT OF THINGS, LIS. I KNOW THAT MILHOUSE WILL SOMEDAY SUFFER FROM MALE PATTERN BALDNESS. I KNOW THAT LUNCHLADY DORIS'S MEATLOAF CONTAINS NEITHER MEAT NOR LOAF. AND I KNOW THAT EL BARTO IS INNOCENT.
OKAY, OKAY. CALM DOWN.
LOOK, IT'S UNFAIR FOR THIS EL BARTO... WHO IS DEFINITELY *NOT* ONE OF THE PEOPLE IN THIS ROOM...TO BE BLAMED FOR SOMETHING HE DIDN'T DO. I CAN'T JUST SIT HERE. I'VE GOT TO *DO* SOMETHING.
WHAT HAVE YOU GOT IN MIND?
OKAY, FIRST I FILL PRINCIPAL SKINNER'S PANTS WITH LIVE HAMSTERS, THEN I PUMP HAMSTER FOOD INTO GROUNDSKEEPER WILLIE'S BAGPIPES, AND THE REST PRETTY MUCH WRITES ITSELF.
BUT HOW WILL THAT CLEAR EL BARTO'S REPUTATION?
WHO SAID ANYTHING ABOUT CLEARING HIS REPUTATION? I'M JUST LOOKING TO BLOW OFF SOME STEAM.

WELL, WE *COULD* DO THAT THING YOU JUST MENTIONED. *OR* WE COULD LAY THE PERFECT TRAP AND GET THE *REAL* CULPRIT TO COME OUT OF HIDING.

HMM...I DUNNO. CAN IT INVOLVE HAMSTERS? IF NOT, I GOTTA SAY, I'M KINDA ON THE FENCE.

BART!!

OKAY, OKAY. WE'LL PLAN YOUR STUPID TRAP-THING.

SO WHAT'S YOUR BIG IDEA?

ALL WE NEED IS A PICTURE OF A FACE BIG ENOUGH TO FIT ON A BILLBOARD, AND IT CAN'T ALREADY HAVE BEEN VANDALIZED BY THE MUSTACHE DOODLER.

A FACE, EH? YOU LEAVE THAT TO ME...

THE FOLLOWING DAY...

WELL, WHOEVER THE MUSTACHE DOODLER IS, HE WON'T BE ABLE TO RESIST *THIS!*

BUT WHERE DID YOU GET THAT GIANT PICTURE OF MRS. KRABAPPEL?

NOW THE SPRINGFIELD ART MUSEUM: TWISTED & SURREAL! THE WOMEN OF PICASSO

UH, YOU'RE BETTER OFF NOT KNOWING, LIS.

MEANWHILE, AT PRINCIPAL SKINNER'S HOUSE...

EDNA

:SIGH: EVEN YOUR *PICTURES* ARE ABANDONING ME, EDNA.

BACK AT THE TOWN SQUARE...

IT'S ALMOST PERFECT.

ALMOST...?

WE JUST NEED TO ADD ONE FINAL TOUCH.

MOMENTS LATER...

WHAT ARE YOU DOING?

THERE. *NOW* IT'S PERFECT.

OBSERVE: THE MUSTACHE DOODLER COMES NEAR THE BILLBOARD, SETTING OFF THE TRIP WIRE. A RAIN OF JELL-O FALLS ON HIS STUPID HEAD. WHAT'S THAT, YOU SAY? IT'S BRILLIANT? STOP, YOU'RE EMBARRASSING ME.

HEY, ISN'T THAT WHAT YOU DID TO MARTIN IN SCHOOL LAST WEEK?

WHAT CAN I SAY? WHY MESS WITH A CLASSIC?

SURREAL

MATH T
1-800

NOW WHAT?

NOW WE TAKE TURNS GUARDING THE BILLBOARD UNTIL THE CULPRIT SHOWS UP.

OKAY, *YOU* GO FIRST.

NO, *YOU* GO FIRST.

HOURS LATER...

YOU GO ⹂YAWN⹄ FIRST.

NO, ⹂YAWN⹄ *YOU* GO FIRST.

AND, BY NIGHTTIME...

ZZZZZZZZ

SPLORCH!!

AAAGHH!!

WHA--?!

THE END

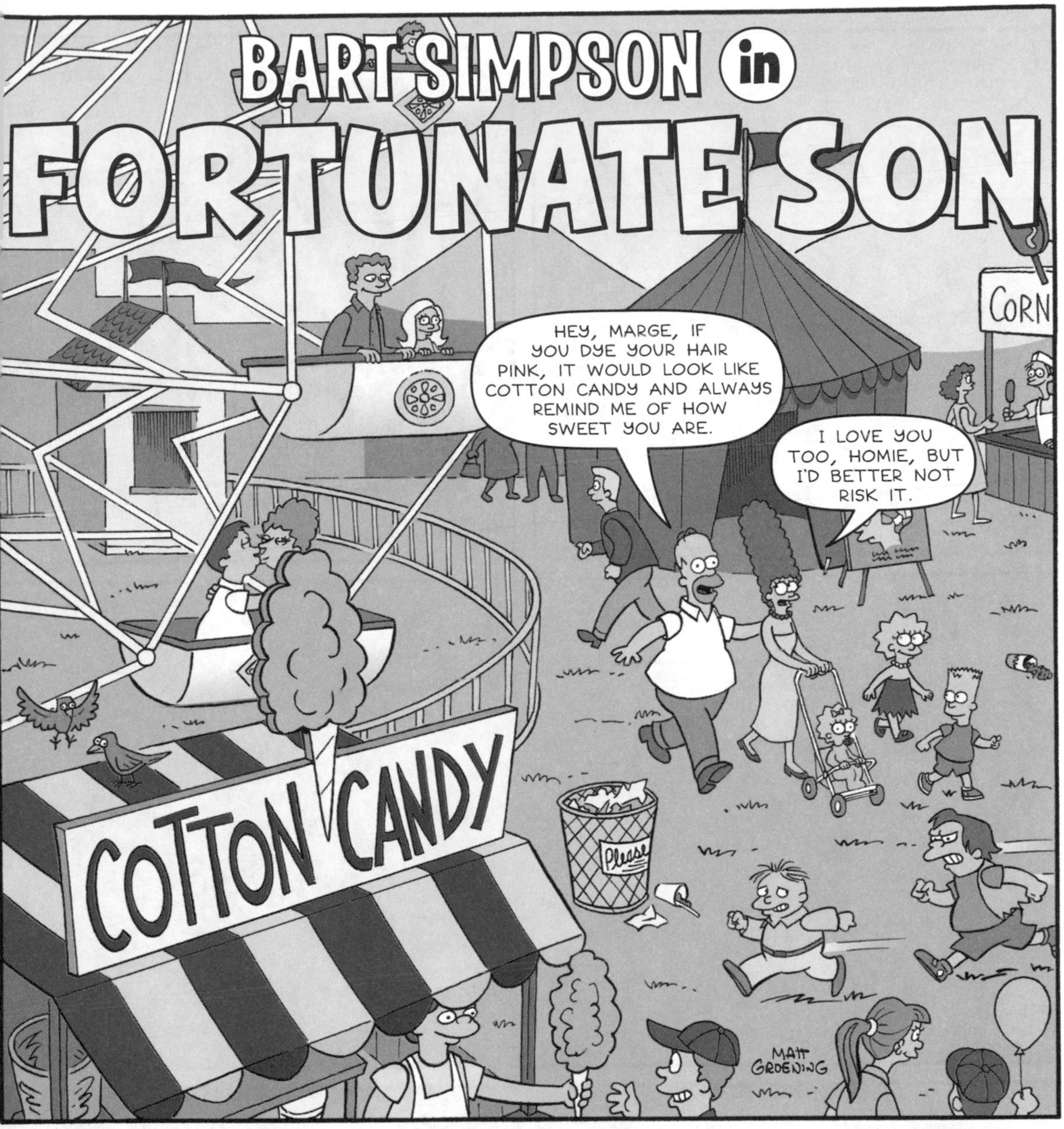
BART SIMPSON in
FORTUNATE SON
CORN
HEY, MARGE, IF YOU DYE YOUR HAIR PINK, IT WOULD LOOK LIKE COTTON CANDY AND ALWAYS REMIND ME OF HOW SWEET YOU ARE.
I LOVE YOU TOO, HOMIE, BUT I'D BETTER NOT RISK IT.
COTTON CANDY
Please
MATT GROENING

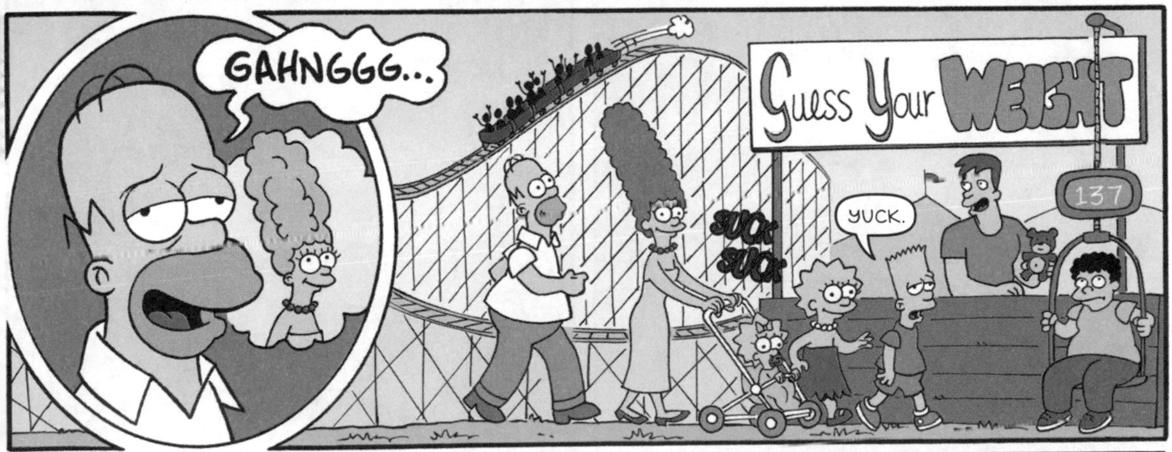
GAHNGGG...
Guess Your WEIGHT
137
SUCK SUCK
YUCK.

CAROL LAY	ART VILLANUEVA	KAREN BATES	BILL MORRISON
STORY & ART	COLORS	LETTERS	EDITOR

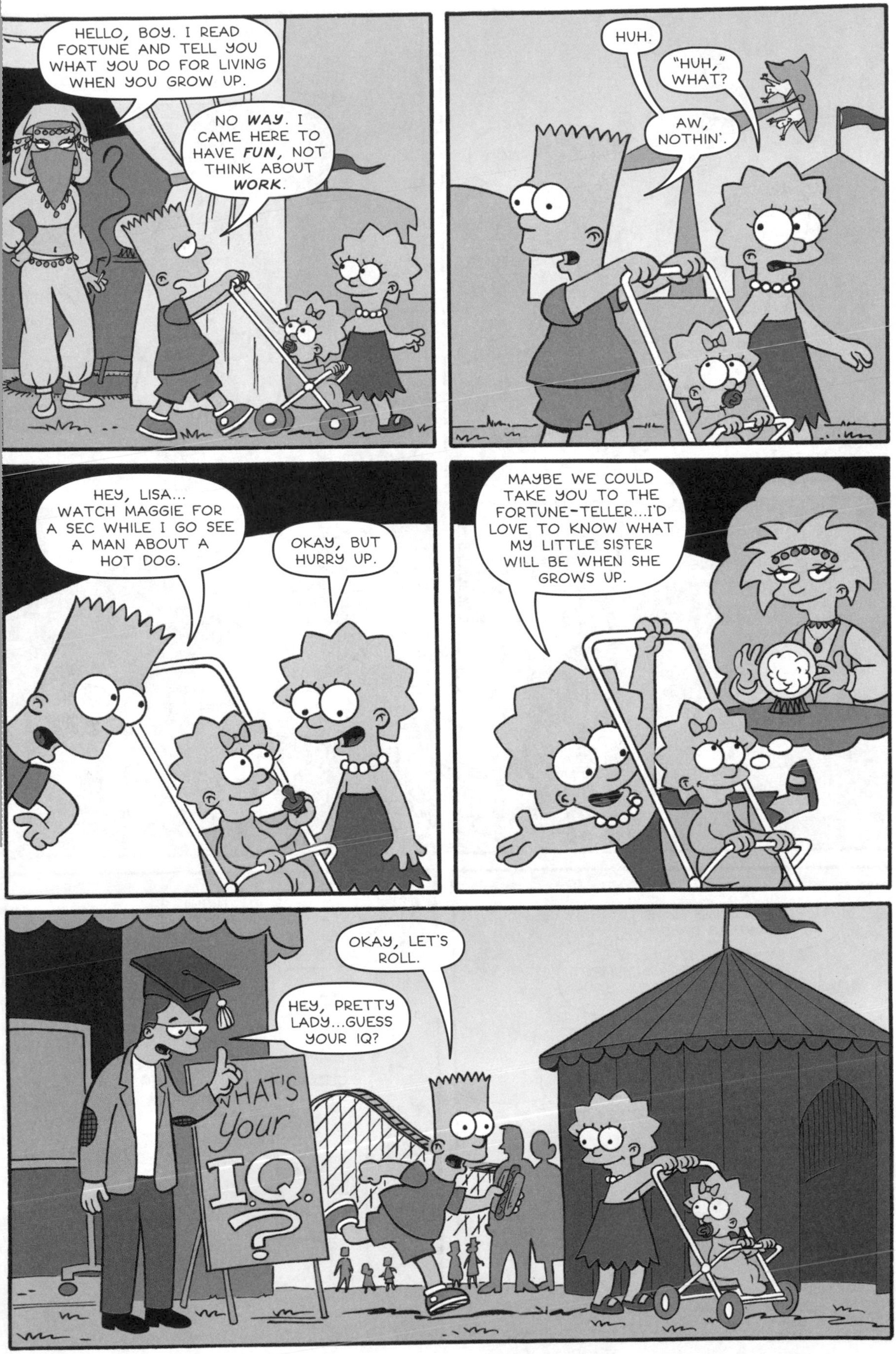
HELLO, BOY. I READ FORTUNE AND TELL YOU WHAT YOU DO FOR LIVING WHEN YOU GROW UP.
NO WAY. I CAME HERE TO HAVE FUN, NOT THINK ABOUT WORK.
HUH.
"HUH," WHAT?
AW, NOTHIN'.
HEY, LISA... WATCH MAGGIE FOR A SEC WHILE I GO SEE A MAN ABOUT A HOT DOG.
OKAY, BUT HURRY UP.
MAYBE WE COULD TAKE YOU TO THE FORTUNE-TELLER...I'D LOVE TO KNOW WHAT MY LITTLE SISTER WILL BE WHEN SHE GROWS UP.
OKAY, LET'S ROLL.
HEY, PRETTY LADY...GUESS YOUR IQ?
WHAT'S Your I.Q.?

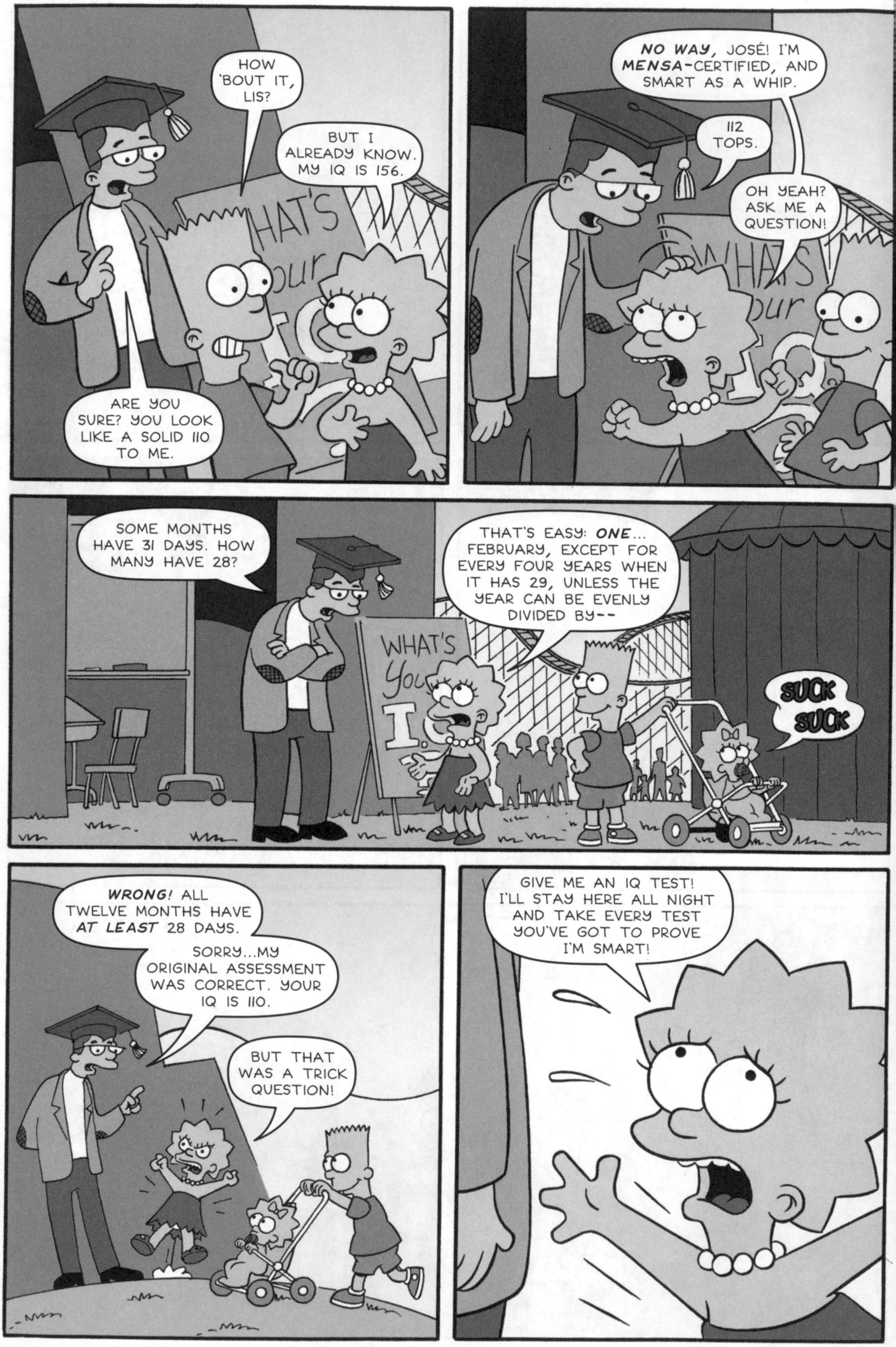

HOW 'BOUT IT, LIS?
BUT I ALREADY KNOW. MY IQ IS 156.
ARE YOU SURE? YOU LOOK LIKE A SOLID 110 TO ME.
NO WAY, JOSÉ! I'M MENSA-CERTIFIED, AND SMART AS A WHIP.
112 TOPS.
OH YEAH? ASK ME A QUESTION!
SOME MONTHS HAVE 31 DAYS. HOW MANY HAVE 28?
THAT'S EASY: ONE... FEBRUARY, EXCEPT FOR EVERY FOUR YEARS WHEN IT HAS 29, UNLESS THE YEAR CAN BE EVENLY DIVIDED BY--
SUCK SUCK
WRONG! ALL TWELVE MONTHS HAVE AT LEAST 28 DAYS.
SORRY...MY ORIGINAL ASSESSMENT WAS CORRECT. YOUR IQ IS 110.
BUT THAT WAS A TRICK QUESTION!
GIVE ME AN IQ TEST! I'LL STAY HERE ALL NIGHT AND TAKE EVERY TEST YOU'VE GOT TO PROVE I'M SMART!

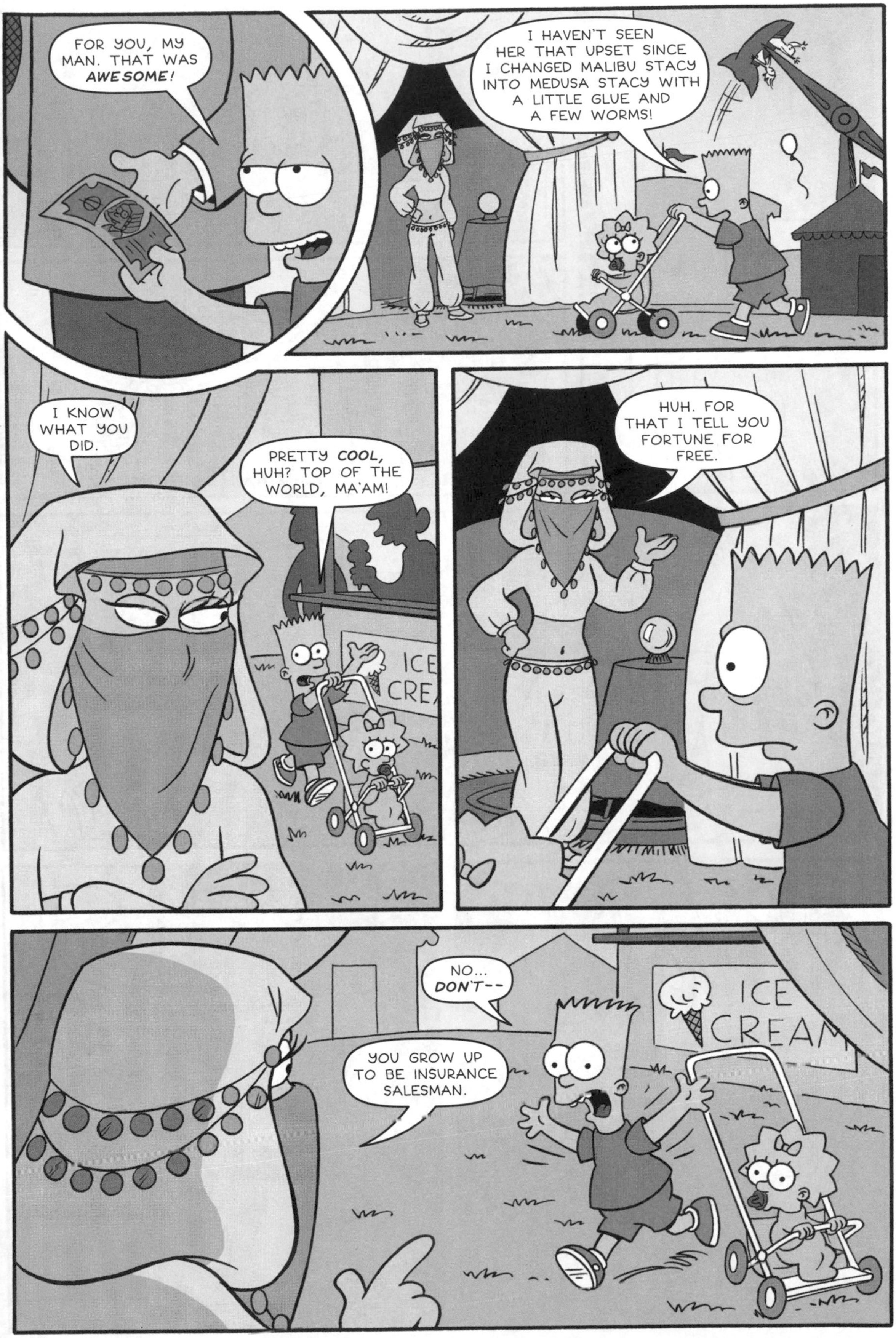

FOR YOU, MY MAN. THAT WAS **AWESOME**!
I HAVEN'T SEEN HER THAT UPSET SINCE I CHANGED MALIBU STACY INTO MEDUSA STACY WITH A LITTLE GLUE AND A FEW WORMS!
I KNOW WHAT YOU DID.
PRETTY **COOL**, HUH? TOP OF THE WORLD, MA'AM!
ICE CREA
HUH. FOR THAT I TELL YOU FORTUNE FOR FREE.
NO... **DON'T**--
ICE CREAM
YOU GROW UP TO BE INSURANCE SALESMAN.

THE END

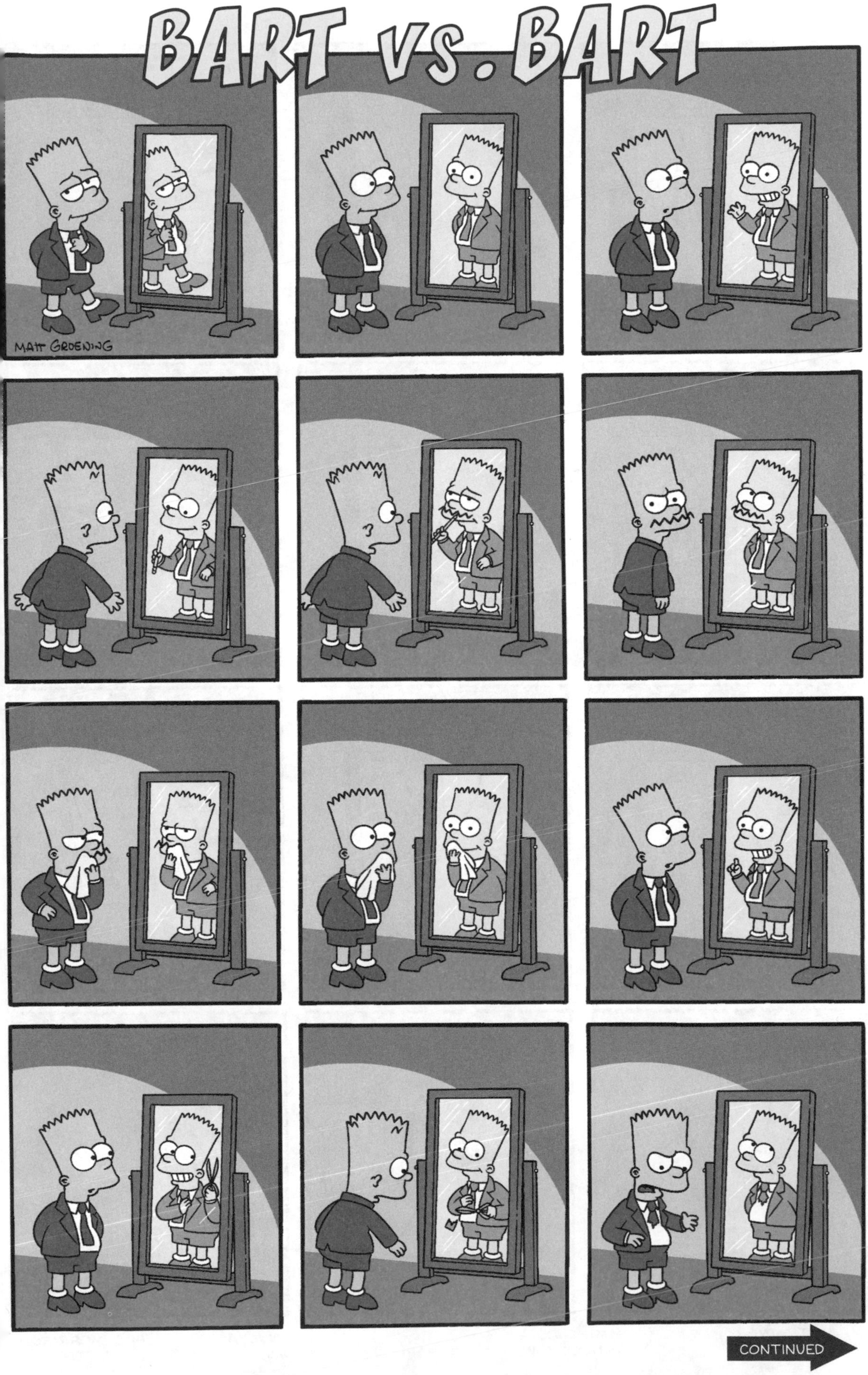
BART VS. BART
MATT GROENING
CONTINUED

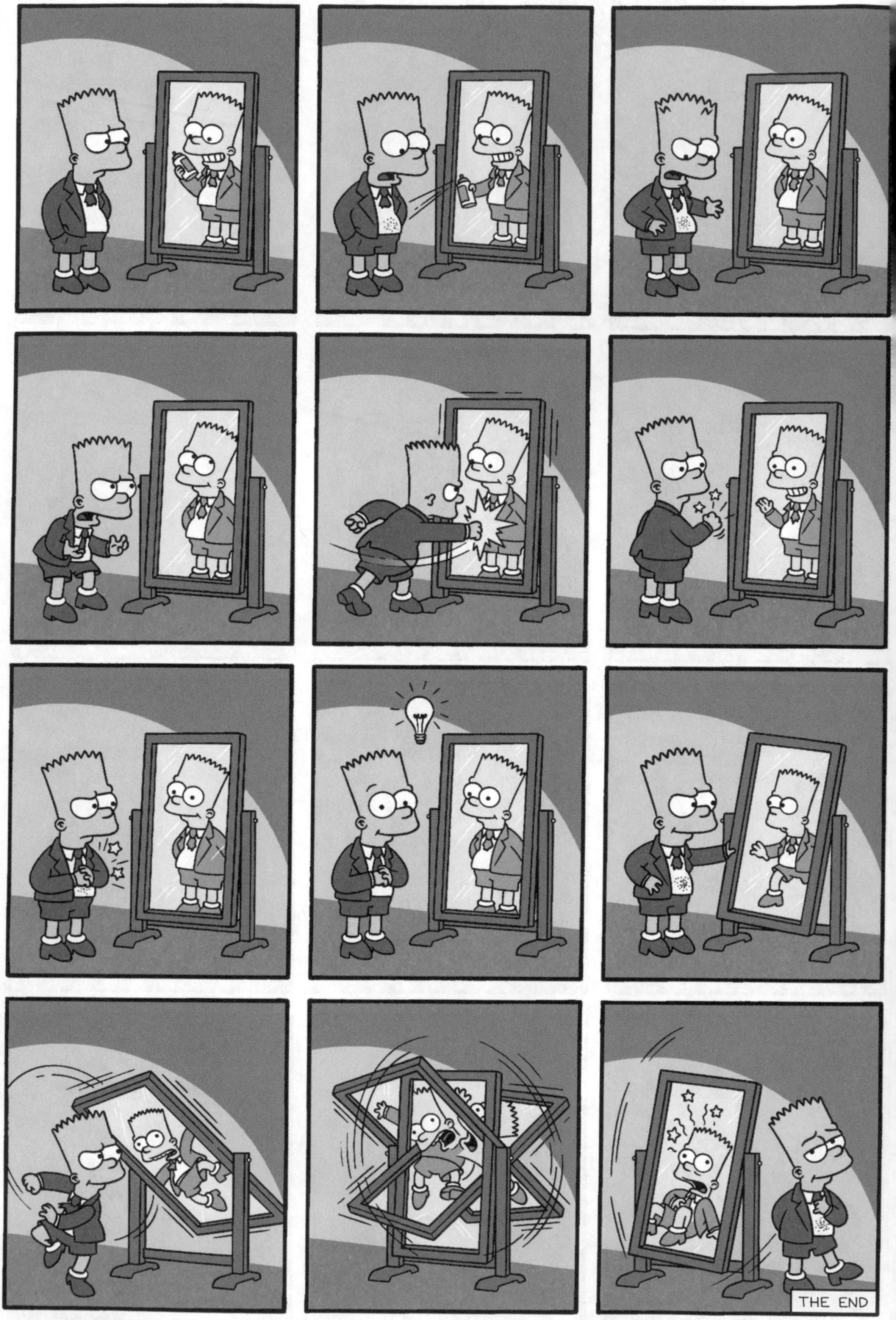
THE END

MARY TRAINOR
STORY & LAYOUTS

MIKE ROTE
PENCILS & INKS

ART VILLANUEVA
COLORS

BILL MORRISON
EDITOR

MAGGIE'S CRIB

by ARAGONÉS

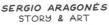

SERGIO ARAGONÉS
STORY & ART

ART VILLANUEVA
COLORS

BILL MORRISON
EDITOR

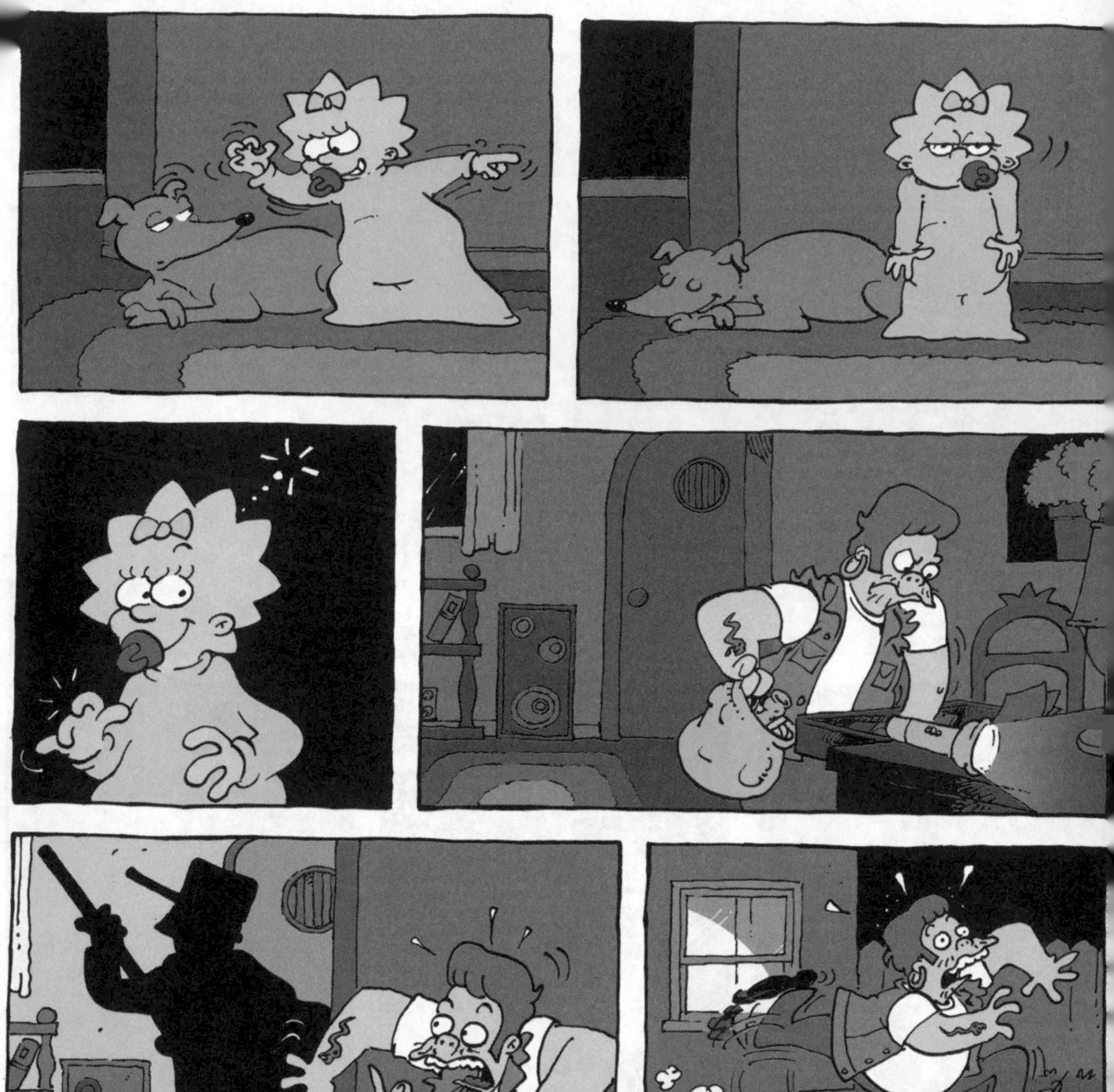
ARAGONES 09

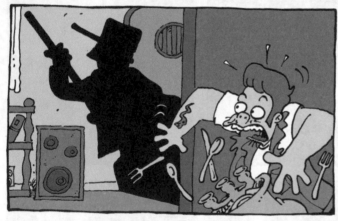

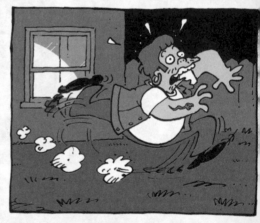

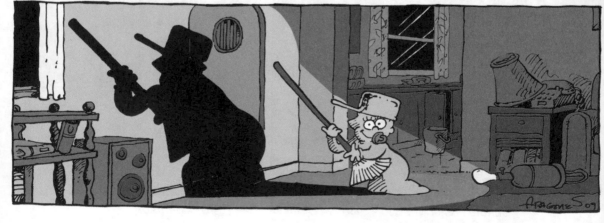

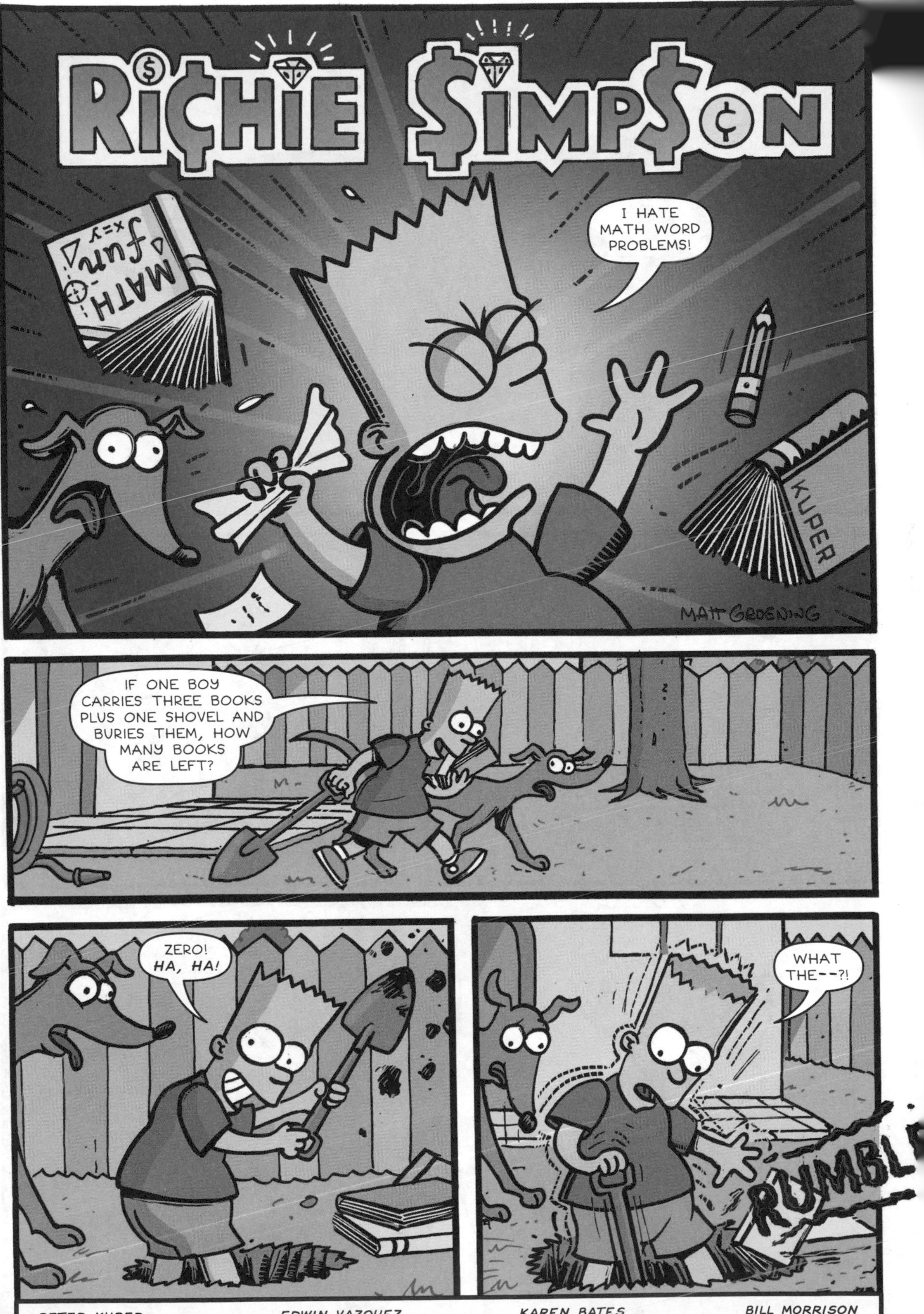

RI¢HIE IMP¢ON
MATH fun x=y
I HATE MATH WORD PROBLEMS!
KUPER
MATT GROENING
IF ONE BOY CARRIES THREE BOOKS PLUS ONE SHOVEL AND BURIES THEM, HOW MANY BOOKS ARE LEFT?
ZERO! *HA, HA!*
WHAT THE--?!
RUMBLE

PETER KUPER SCRIPT & ART · **EDWIN VAZQUEZ** COLORS · **KAREN BATES** LETTERS · **BILL MORRISON** EDITOR

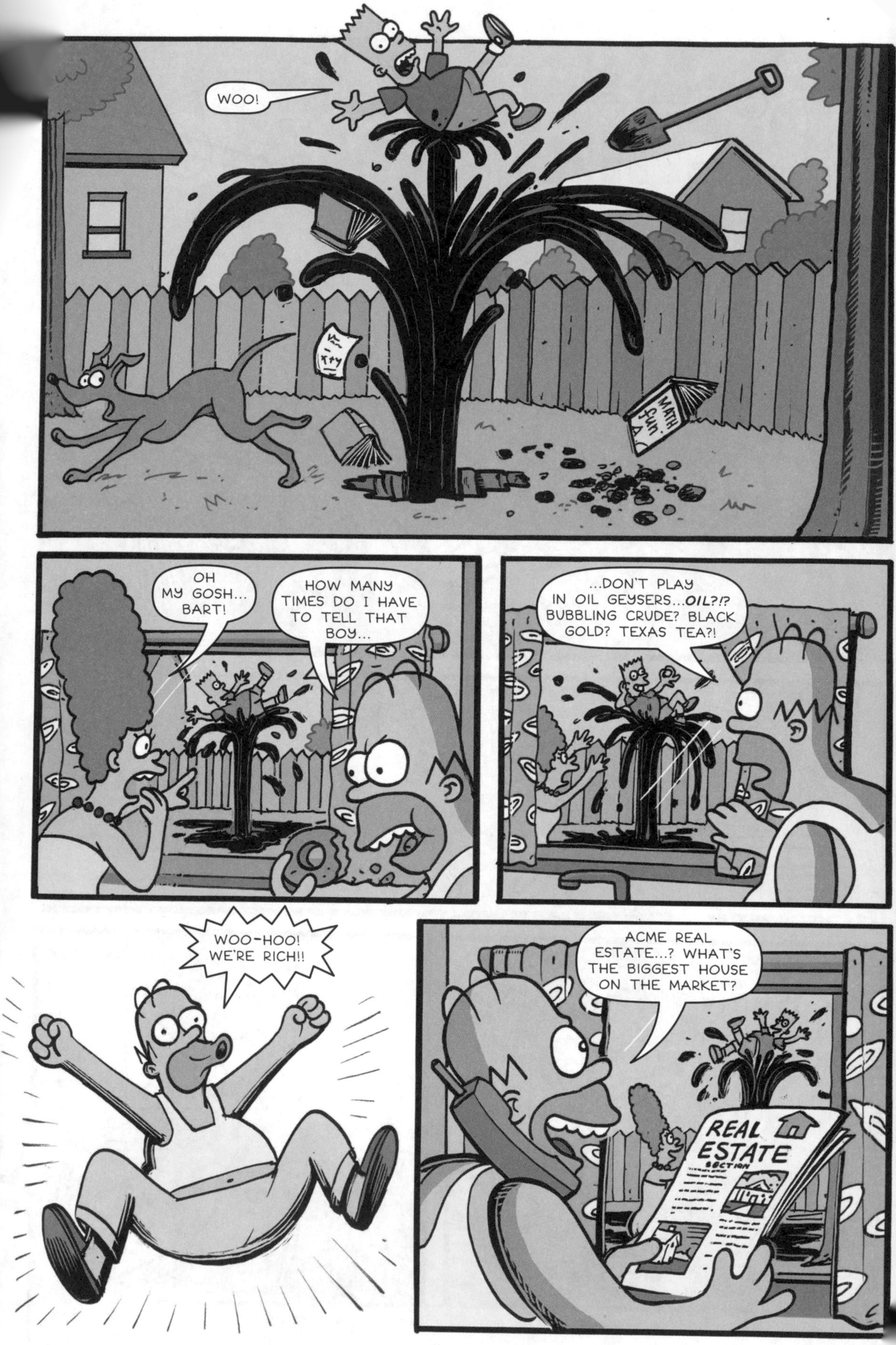
WOO!
MATH fun!
OH MY GOSH... BART!
HOW MANY TIMES DO I HAVE TO TELL THAT BOY...
...DON'T PLAY IN OIL GEYSERS...OIL?!? BUBBLING CRUDE? BLACK GOLD? TEXAS TEA?!
WOO-HOO! WE'RE RICH!!
ACME REAL ESTATE...? WHAT'S THE BIGGEST HOUSE ON THE MARKET?
REAL ESTATE SECTION

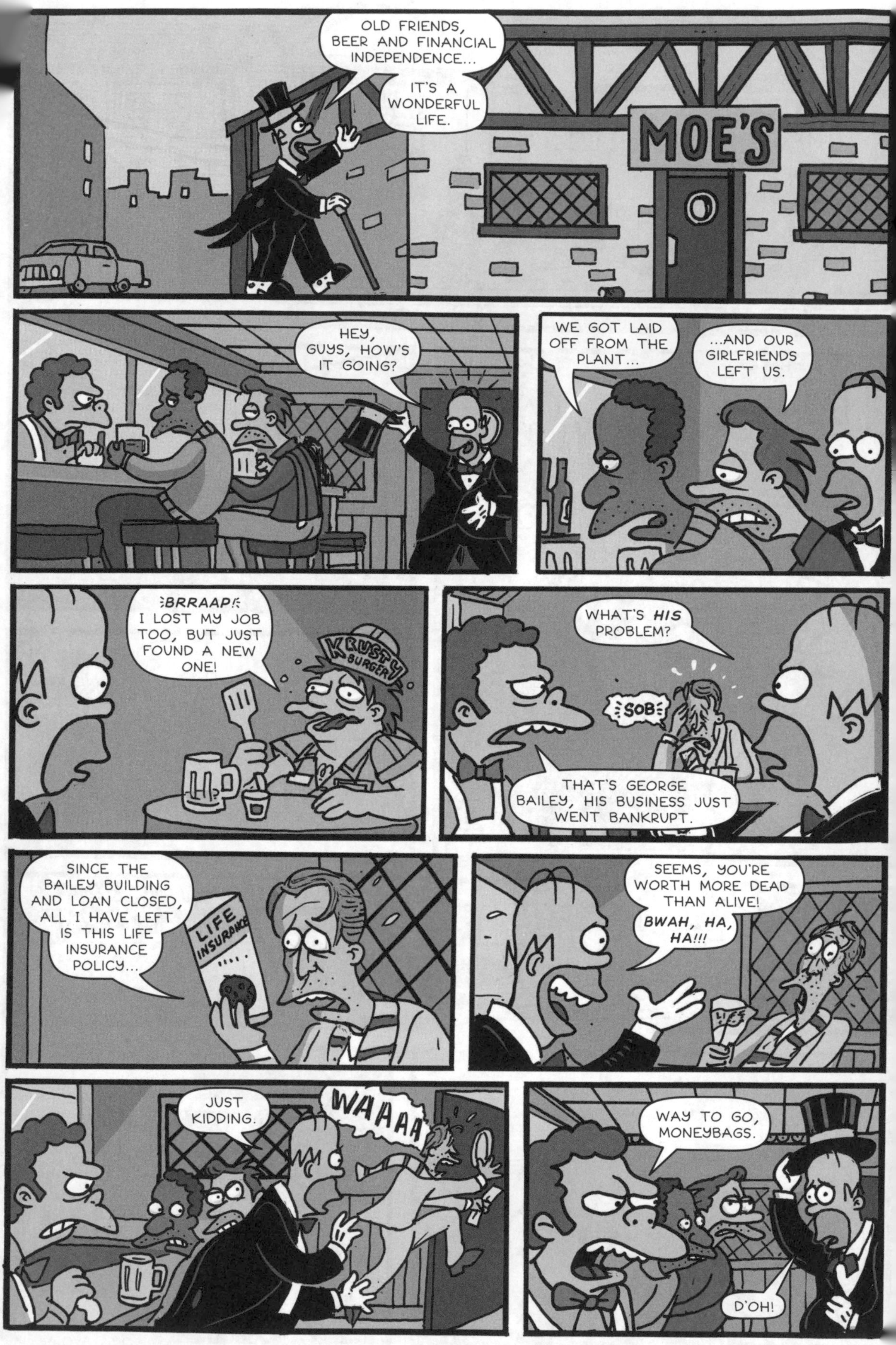
OLD FRIENDS, BEER AND FINANCIAL INDEPENDENCE...
IT'S A WONDERFUL LIFE.
MOE'S
HEY, GUYS, HOW'S IT GOING?
WE GOT LAID OFF FROM THE PLANT...
...AND OUR GIRLFRIENDS LEFT US.
BRRAAP!
I LOST MY JOB TOO, BUT JUST FOUND A NEW ONE!
KRUSTY BURGER
WHAT'S HIS PROBLEM?
SOB
THAT'S GEORGE BAILEY, HIS BUSINESS JUST WENT BANKRUPT.
SINCE THE BAILEY BUILDING AND LOAN CLOSED, ALL I HAVE LEFT IS THIS LIFE INSURANCE POLICY...
LIFE INSURANCE
SEEMS, YOU'RE WORTH MORE DEAD THAN ALIVE!
BWAH, HA, HA!!!
JUST KIDDING.
WAAAAA
WAY TO GO, MONEYBAGS.
D'OH!

THE PLASTIC SURGEON SAYS ONE MORE LIFT SHOULD DO IT...

...MY PSYCHIATRIST THINKS I NEED TO INCREASE MY DOSAGE...

YOU KNOW, MARGE, YOU SHOULD REALLY CONSIDER BOTOX...

Springfield Country Club®
◄ NO RIFF-RAFF ►
SINCE 1981

REALLY! IT'LL WIPE AWAY YEARS.

HMM...I DON'T KNOW.

HERE YOU GO, LADIES...THREE TRIPLE MARTINIS...

...AND ONE SHIRLEY TEMPLE.

I-I'M WATCHING MY FIGURE.

MARGE, YOU'VE GOT TO LAY OFF THOSE KID DRINKS.

SPEAKING OF KIDS, HAVE I SHOWN YOU MINE?

MY ARTHUR IS BACK IN REHAB.

TIFFANY'S THERAPIST SAYS HER SUICIDE ATTEMPTS ARE JUST AN ATTENTION GETTING DEVICE.

I'M CONSIDERING PUTTING MY LITTLE ZANE ON MUCH STRONGER ANTI-DEPRESSANTS.

AT LEAST THEY AREN'T IN OUR HAIR!

THANK GOODNESS FOR BOARDING SCHOOLS.

AMEN!

HRMMM...

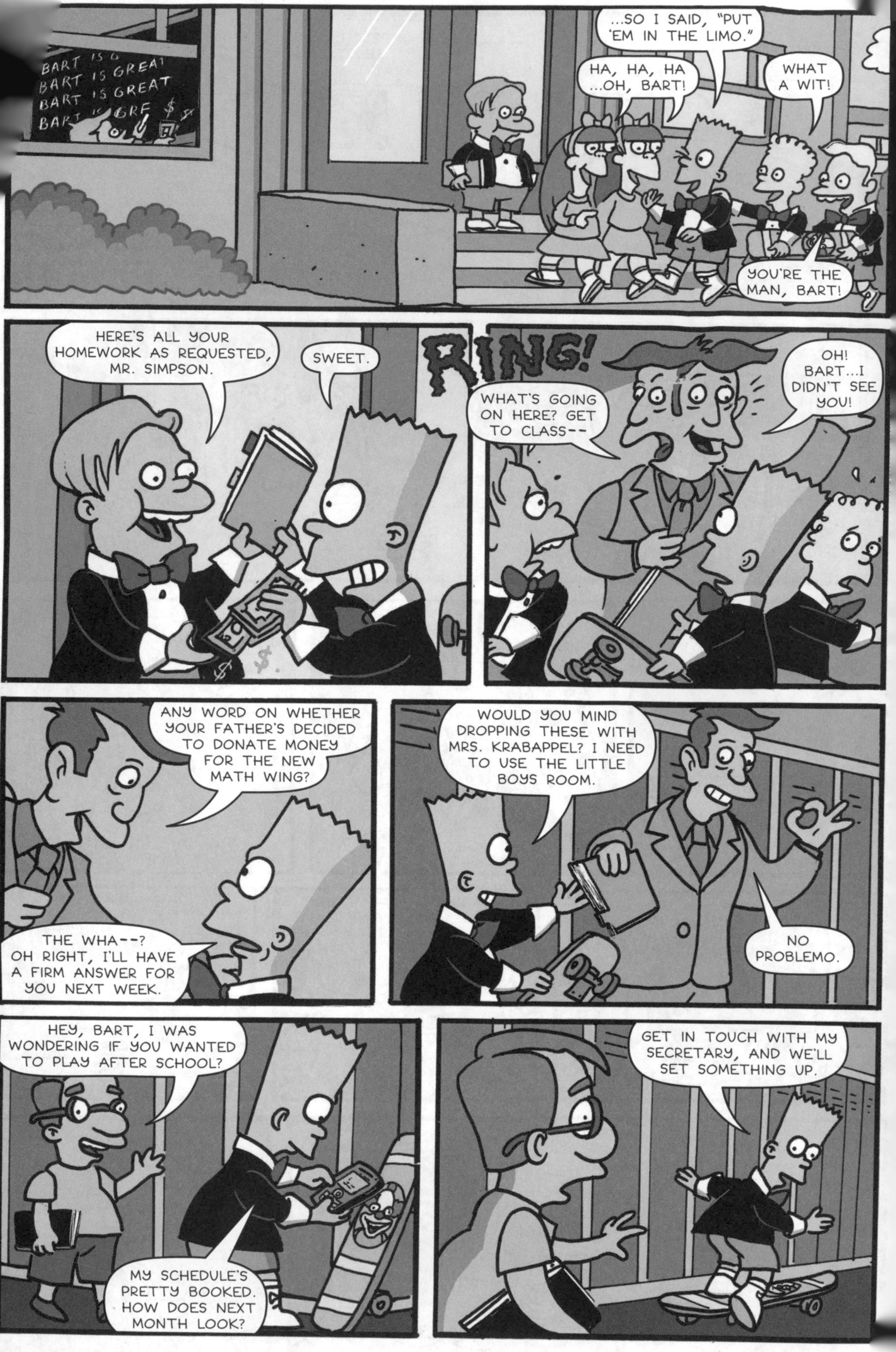
BART IS G
BART IS GREAT
BART IS GREAT
BART IS GRE
...SO I SAID, "PUT 'EM IN THE LIMO."
HA, HA, HA ...OH, BART!
WHAT A WIT!
YOU'RE THE MAN, BART!
HERE'S ALL YOUR HOMEWORK AS REQUESTED, MR. SIMPSON.
SWEET.
RING!
WHAT'S GOING ON HERE? GET TO CLASS--
OH! BART...I DIDN'T SEE YOU!
ANY WORD ON WHETHER YOUR FATHER'S DECIDED TO DONATE MONEY FOR THE NEW MATH WING?
THE WHA--? OH RIGHT, I'LL HAVE A FIRM ANSWER FOR YOU NEXT WEEK.
WOULD YOU MIND DROPPING THESE WITH MRS. KRABAPPEL? I NEED TO USE THE LITTLE BOYS ROOM.
NO PROBLEMO.
HEY, BART, I WAS WONDERING IF YOU WANTED TO PLAY AFTER SCHOOL?
MY SCHEDULE'S PRETTY BOOKED. HOW DOES NEXT MONTH LOOK?
GET IN TOUCH WITH MY SECRETARY, AND WE'LL SET SOMETHING UP.

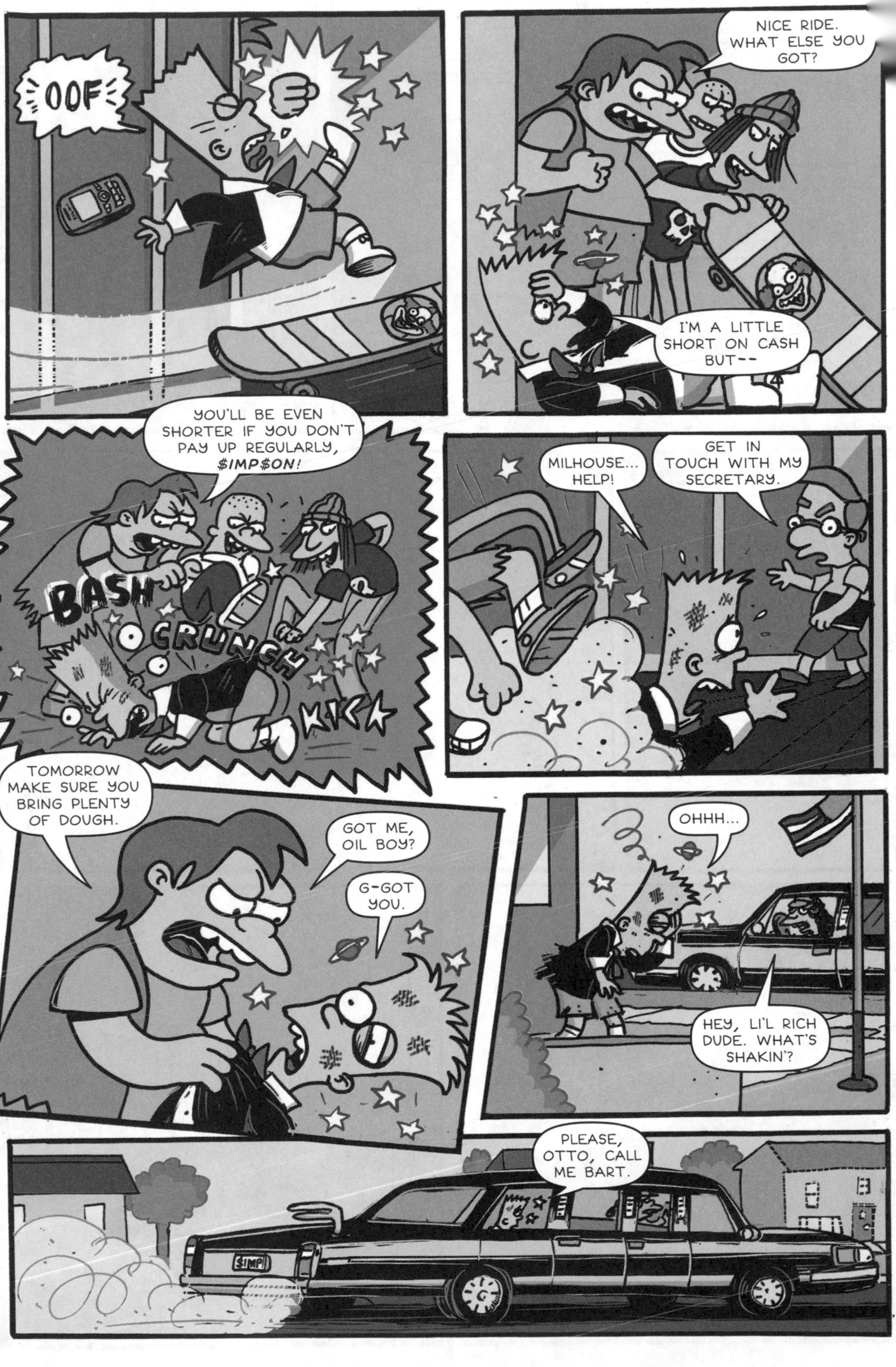
OOF
NICE RIDE. WHAT ELSE YOU GOT?
I'M A LITTLE SHORT ON CASH BUT--
YOU'LL BE EVEN SHORTER IF YOU DON'T PAY UP REGULARLY, IMPON!
BASH
CRUNCH
KICK
MILHOUSE... HELP!
GET IN TOUCH WITH MY SECRETARY.
TOMORROW MAKE SURE YOU BRING PLENTY OF DOUGH.
GOT ME, OIL BOY?
G-GOT YOU.
OHHH...
HEY, LI'L RICH DUDE. WHAT'S SHAKIN'?
PLEASE, OTTO, CALL ME BART.
$IMP

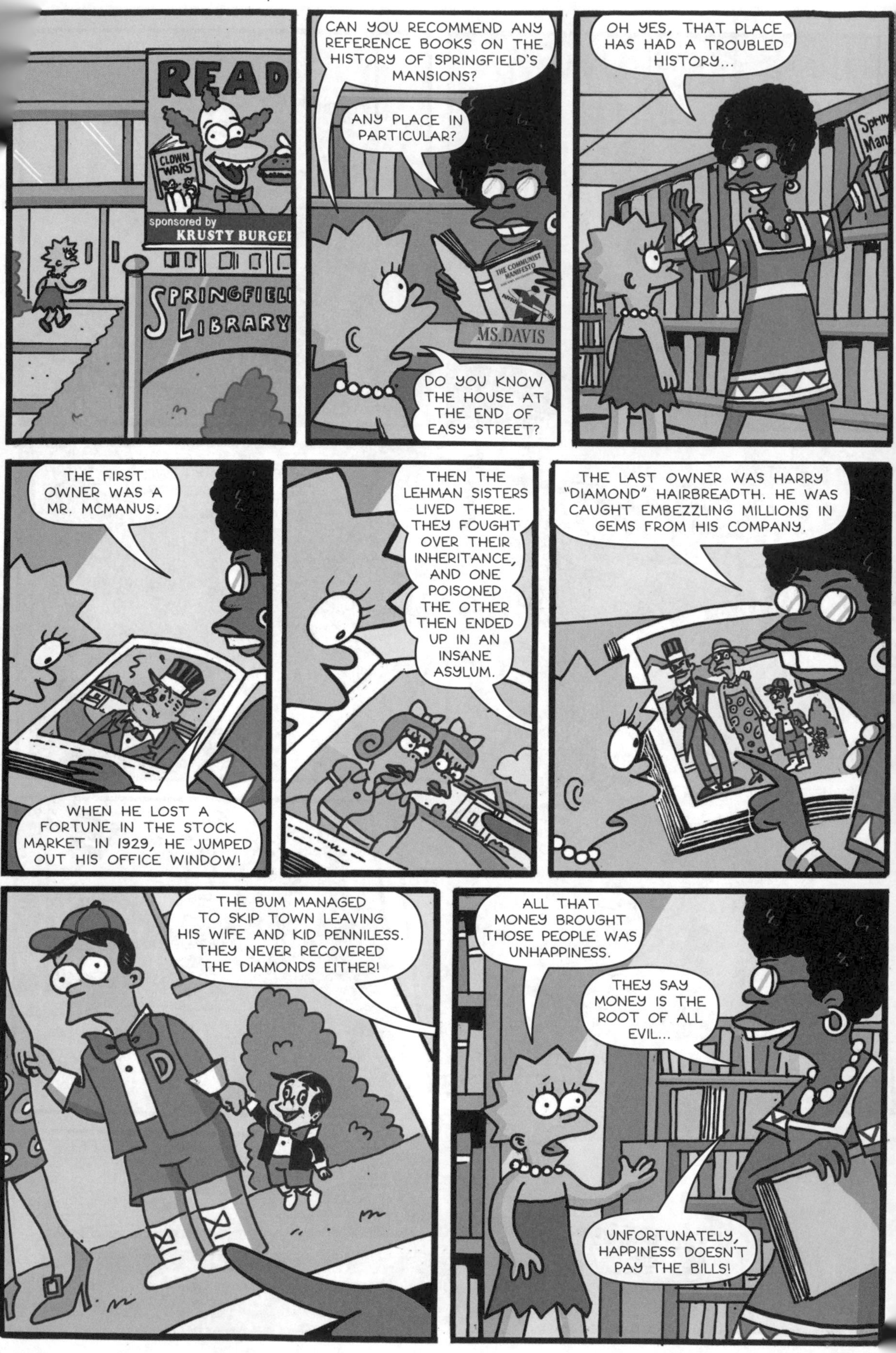
READ
CLOWN WARS
sponsored by KRUSTY BURGER
SPRINGFIELD LIBRARY
CAN YOU RECOMMEND ANY REFERENCE BOOKS ON THE HISTORY OF SPRINGFIELD'S MANSIONS?
ANY PLACE IN PARTICULAR?
THE COMMUNIST MANIFESTO
MS.DAVIS
DO YOU KNOW THE HOUSE AT THE END OF EASY STREET?
OH YES, THAT PLACE HAS HAD A TROUBLED HISTORY...
THE FIRST OWNER WAS A MR. MCMANUS.
WHEN HE LOST A FORTUNE IN THE STOCK MARKET IN 1929, HE JUMPED OUT HIS OFFICE WINDOW!
THEN THE LEHMAN SISTERS LIVED THERE. THEY FOUGHT OVER THEIR INHERITANCE, AND ONE POISONED THE OTHER THEN ENDED UP IN AN INSANE ASYLUM.
THE LAST OWNER WAS HARRY "DIAMOND" HAIRBREADTH. HE WAS CAUGHT EMBEZZLING MILLIONS IN GEMS FROM HIS COMPANY.
THE BUM MANAGED TO SKIP TOWN LEAVING HIS WIFE AND KID PENNILESS. THEY NEVER RECOVERED THE DIAMONDS EITHER!
ALL THAT MONEY BROUGHT THOSE PEOPLE WAS UNHAPPINESS.
THEY SAY MONEY IS THE ROOT OF ALL EVIL...
UNFORTUNATELY, HAPPINESS DOESN'T PAY THE BILLS!

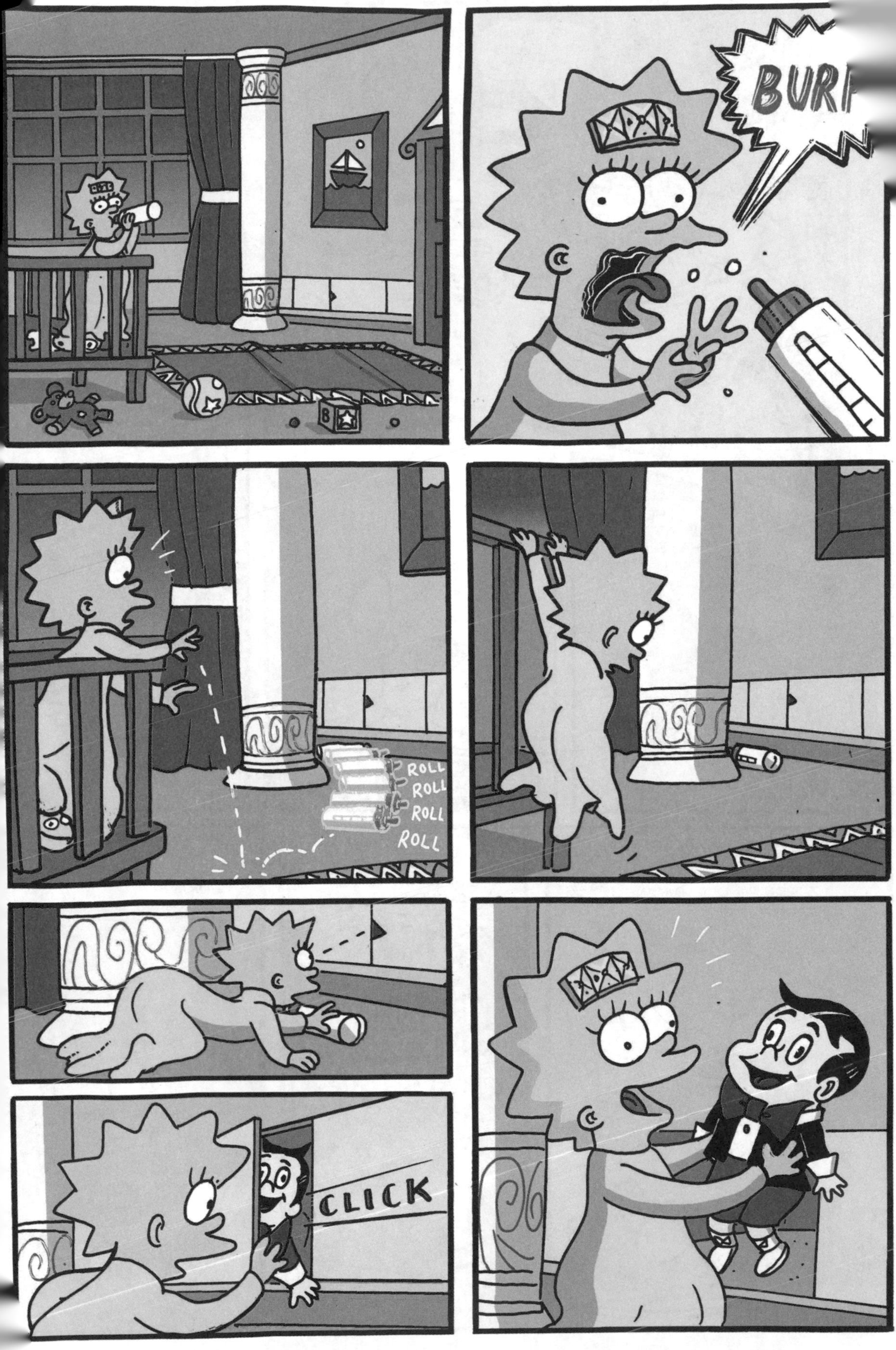
BURP
ROLL
ROLL
ROLL
ROLL
CLICK

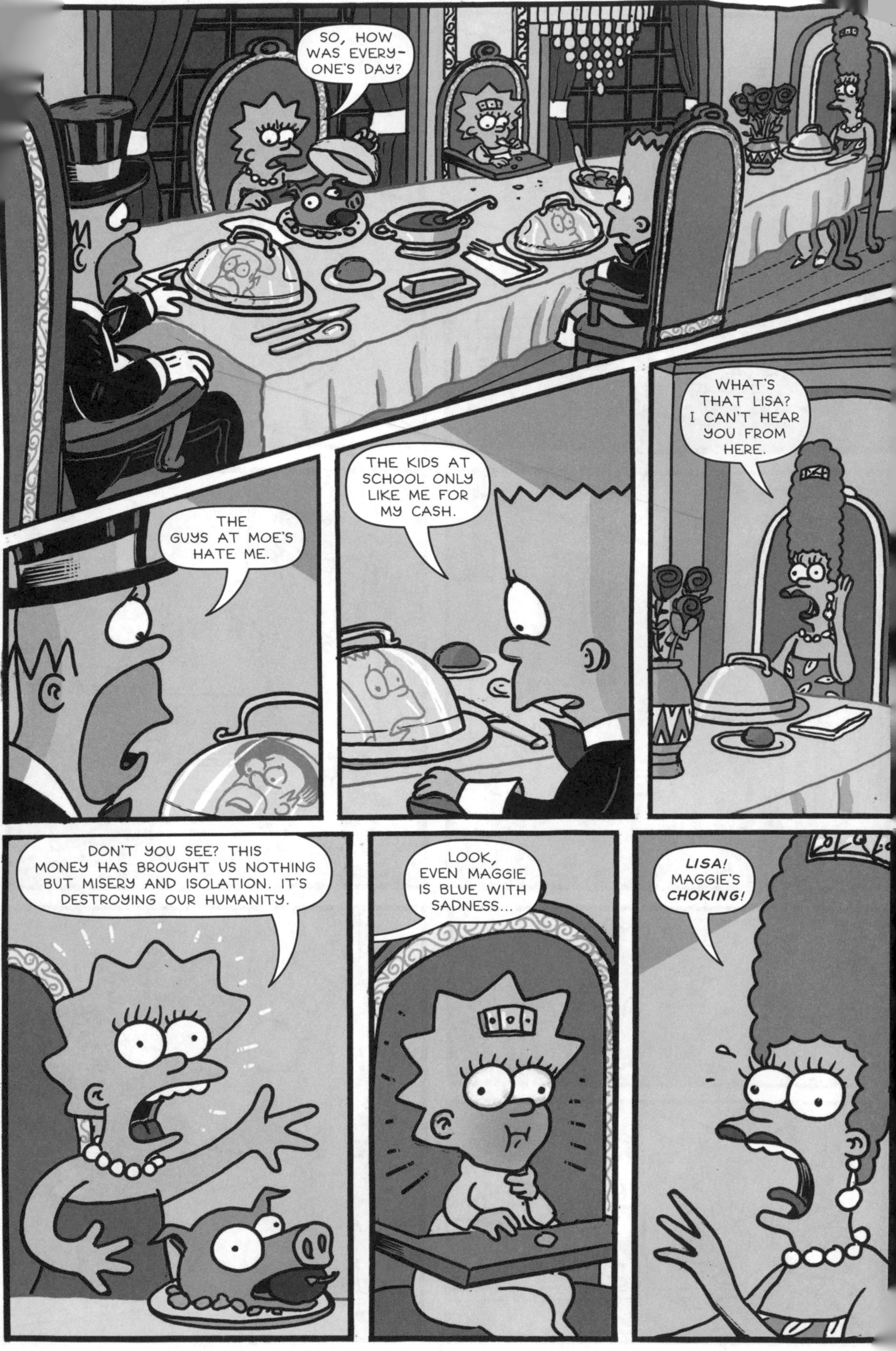
SO, HOW WAS EVERY-ONE'S DAY?
THE GUYS AT MOE'S HATE ME.
THE KIDS AT SCHOOL ONLY LIKE ME FOR MY CASH.
WHAT'S THAT LISA? I CAN'T HEAR YOU FROM HERE.
DON'T YOU SEE? THIS MONEY HAS BROUGHT US NOTHING BUT MISERY AND ISOLATION. IT'S DESTROYING OUR HUMANITY.
LOOK, EVEN MAGGIE IS BLUE WITH SADNESS...
LISA! MAGGIE'S ***CHOKING!***

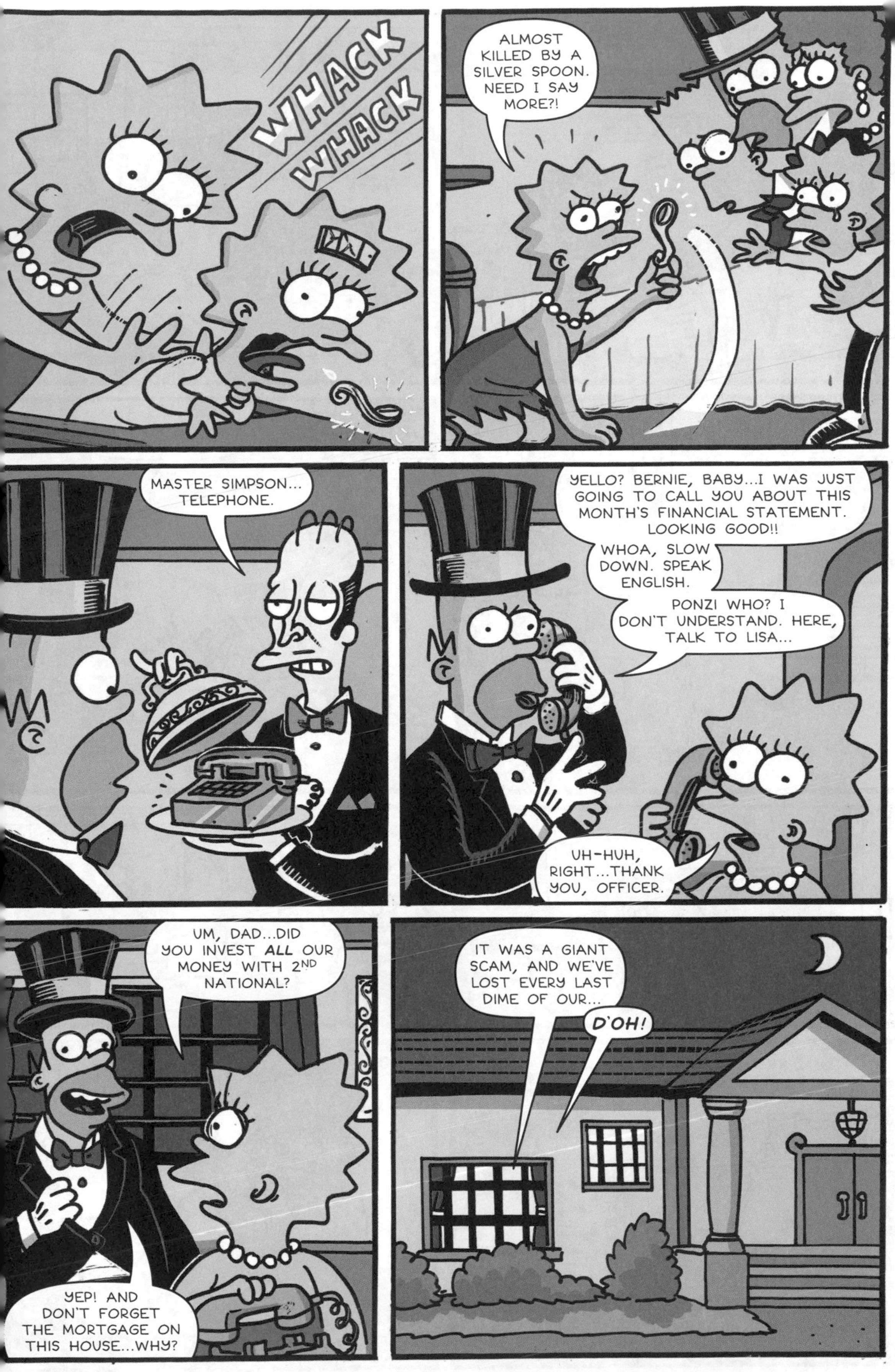
WHACK
WHACK
ALMOST KILLED BY A SILVER SPOON. NEED I SAY MORE?!
MASTER SIMPSON... TELEPHONE.
YELLO? BERNIE, BABY...I WAS JUST GOING TO CALL YOU ABOUT THIS MONTH'S FINANCIAL STATEMENT. LOOKING GOOD!!
WHOA, SLOW DOWN. SPEAK ENGLISH.
PONZI WHO? I DON'T UNDERSTAND. HERE, TALK TO LISA...
UH-HUH, RIGHT...THANK YOU, OFFICER.
UM, DAD...DID YOU INVEST ALL OUR MONEY WITH 2ND NATIONAL?
YEP! AND DON'T FORGET THE MORTGAGE ON THIS HOUSE...WHY?
IT WAS A GIANT SCAM, AND WE'VE LOST EVERY LAST DIME OF OUR...
D'OH!

fin

MAGGIE'S CRIB

by ARAGONES

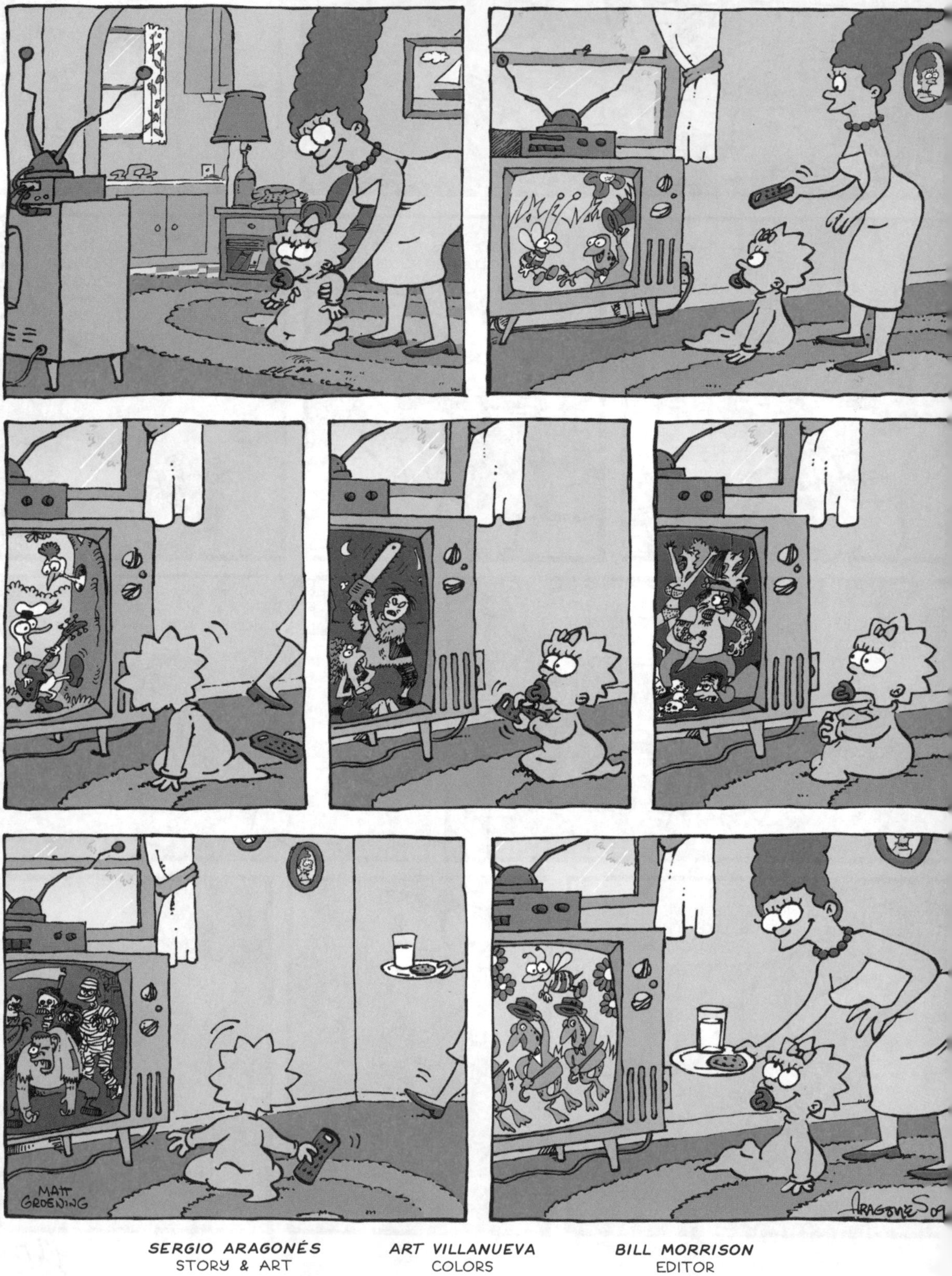
MATT GROENING
ARAGONES 09

SERGIO ARAGONÉS STORY & ART

ART VILLANUEVA COLORS

BILL MORRISON EDITOR

LISA & BART SIMPSON

in

A TOMB WITH A VIEW

CAROL LAY
SCRIPT & ART

NATHAN HAMILL
COLORS

KAREN BATES
LETTERS

BILL MORRISON
EDITOR

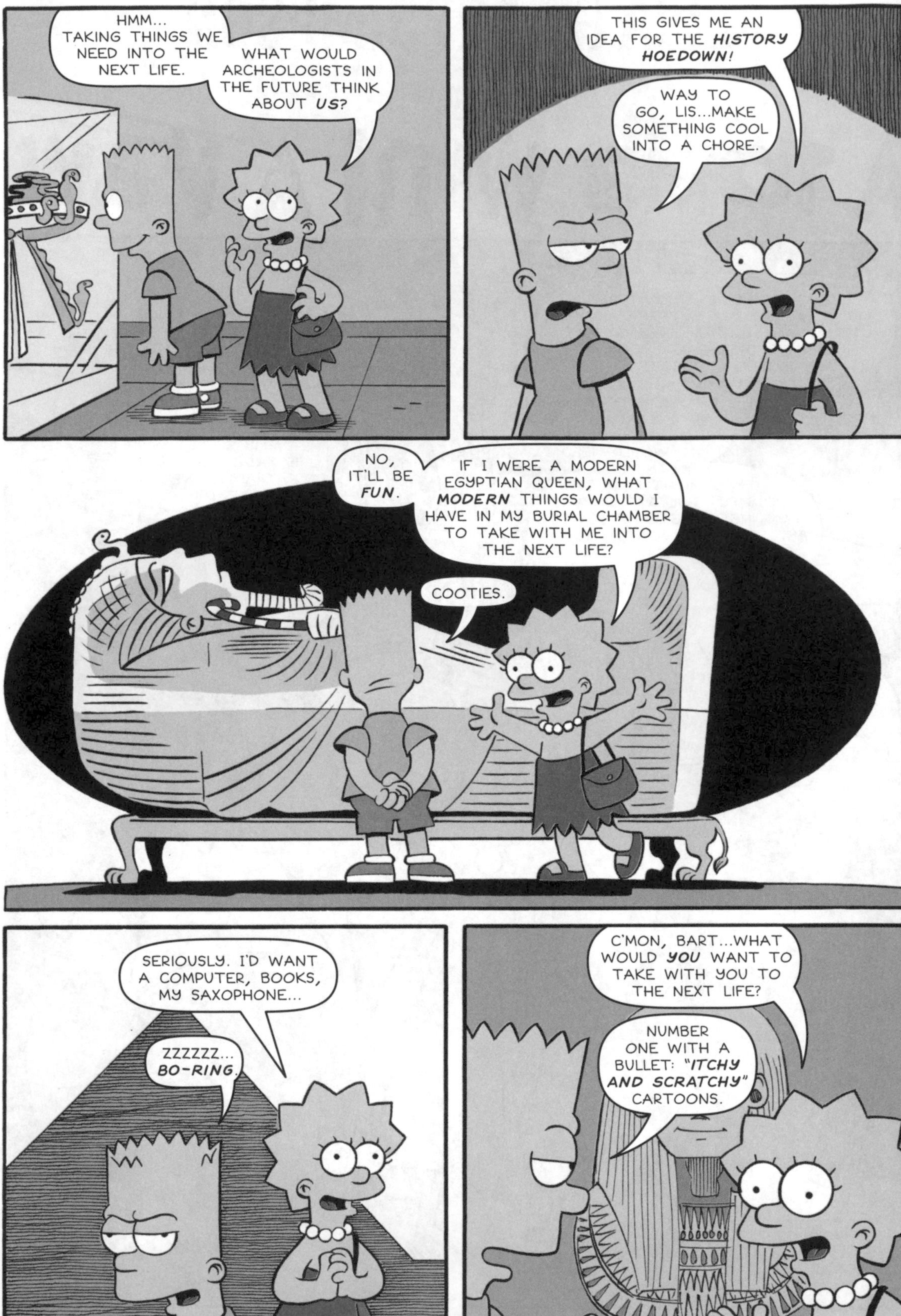
HMM... TAKING THINGS WE NEED INTO THE NEXT LIFE.
WHAT WOULD ARCHEOLOGISTS IN THE FUTURE THINK ABOUT *US*?
THIS GIVES ME AN IDEA FOR THE *HISTORY HOEDOWN*!
WAY TO GO, LIS...MAKE SOMETHING COOL INTO A CHORE.
NO, IT'LL BE *FUN*.
IF I WERE A MODERN EGYPTIAN QUEEN, WHAT *MODERN* THINGS WOULD I HAVE IN MY BURIAL CHAMBER TO TAKE WITH ME INTO THE NEXT LIFE?
COOTIES.
SERIOUSLY. I'D WANT A COMPUTER, BOOKS, MY SAXOPHONE...
ZZZZZZ... *BO-RING*.
C'MON, BART...WHAT WOULD *YOU* WANT TO TAKE WITH YOU TO THE NEXT LIFE?
NUMBER ONE WITH A BULLET: *"ITCHY AND SCRATCHY"* CARTOONS.

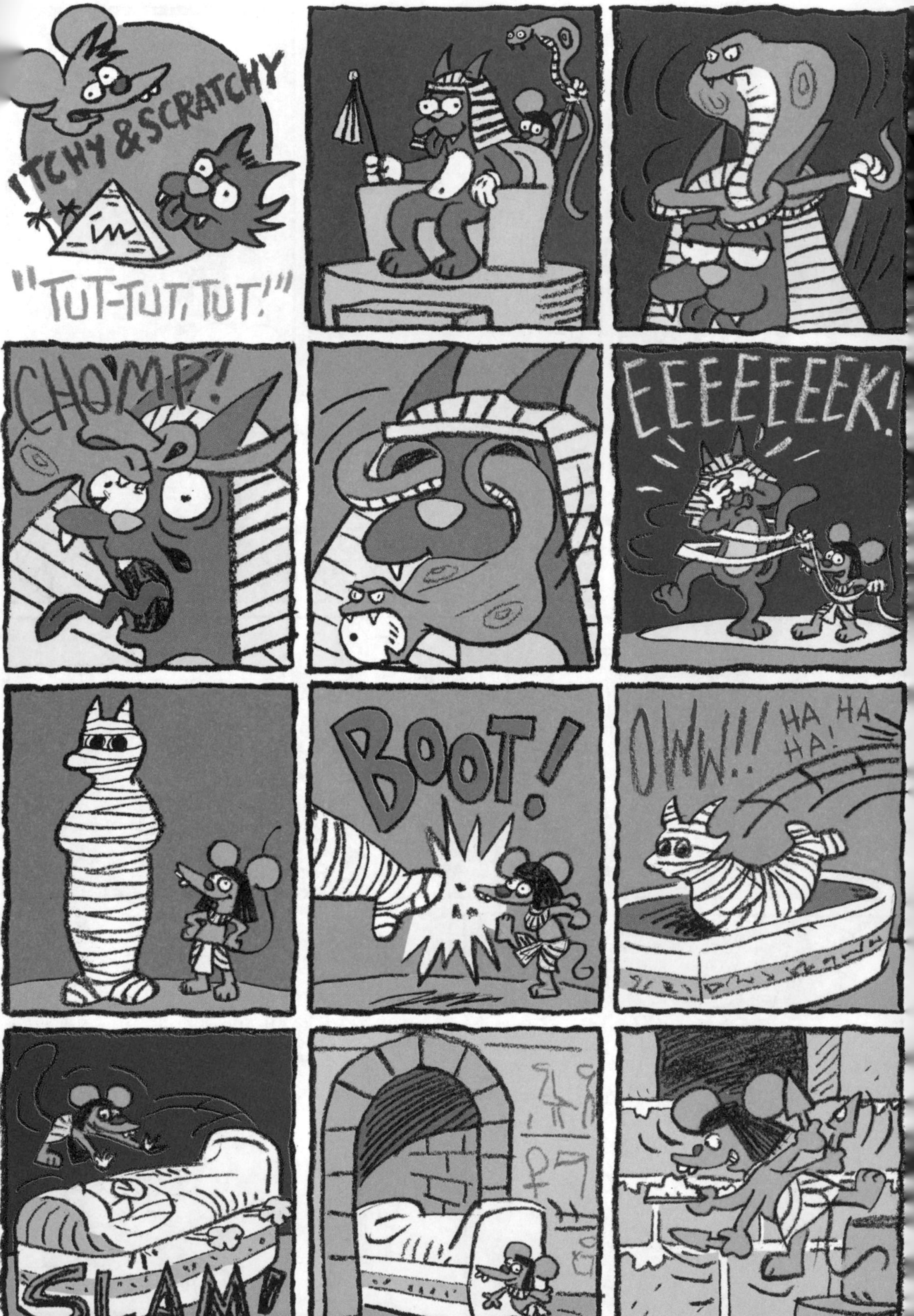
ITCHY & SCRATCHY
in
"TUT-TUT, TUT!"
CHOMP!
EEEEEEEK!
BOOT!
OWW!!
HA HA HA!
SLAM!

SOON...

QUEEN CLEPTOPETRA, PLEASE ENJOY YOUR COMPLETE CLASSICS LIBRARY ALONG WITH YOUR VERY OWN *"ITCHY AND SCRATCHY"* CARTOON ON A GIGANTIC MINIATURE PLASMA SCREEN!

Itchy & Scratchy in "TUT-TUT, TUT!"

OH, THAT'S COMING ALONG SO WELL, LISA! I WOULDN'T BE SURPRISED IF YOU WIN *FIRST PRIZE* AT THE *HISTORY HOEDOWN*.

THANKS, MOM.

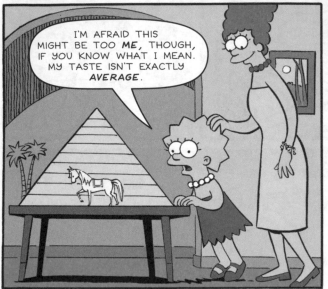

I'M AFRAID THIS MIGHT BE TOO *ME*, THOUGH, IF YOU KNOW WHAT I MEAN. MY TASTE ISN'T EXACTLY *AVERAGE*.

HERE'S SOMETHING A MODERN QUEEN MIGHT ENJOY IN THE NEXT LIFE... A FILIGREED *FAN* IN CASE HER AIR CONDITIONER BREAKS.

GEE, THANKS!

I THINK I'LL ASK OTHER PEOPLE FOR INPUT. I CAN'T THINK OF *EVERYTHING*, YOU KNOW.

♪ QUEEN CLEPTOPETRA, GODDESS OF THE NILE... YOU'VE GOT THE BOOTY THAT MAKES JUDGES SMILE... ♪

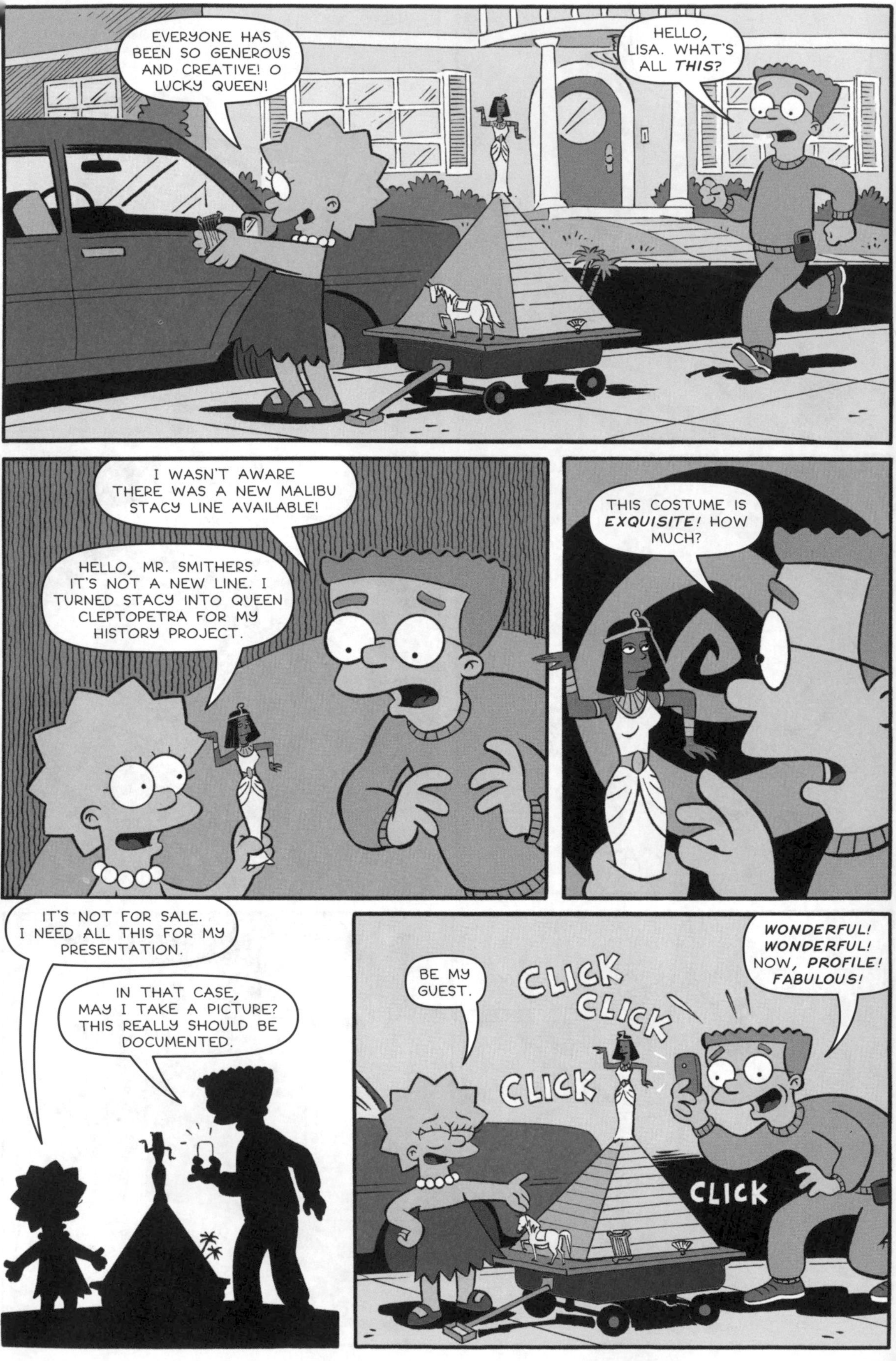
EVERYONE HAS BEEN SO GENEROUS AND CREATIVE! O LUCKY QUEEN!
HELLO, LISA. WHAT'S ALL *THIS*?
I WASN'T AWARE THERE WAS A NEW MALIBU STACY LINE AVAILABLE!
HELLO, MR. SMITHERS. IT'S NOT A NEW LINE. I TURNED STACY INTO QUEEN CLEPTOPETRA FOR MY HISTORY PROJECT.
THIS COSTUME IS *EXQUISITE!* HOW MUCH?
IT'S NOT FOR SALE. I NEED ALL THIS FOR MY PRESENTATION.
IN THAT CASE, MAY I TAKE A PICTURE? THIS REALLY SHOULD BE DOCUMENTED.
BE MY GUEST.
CLICK
CLICK
CLICK
WONDERFUL! WONDERFUL! NOW, *PROFILE! FABULOUS!*
CLICK

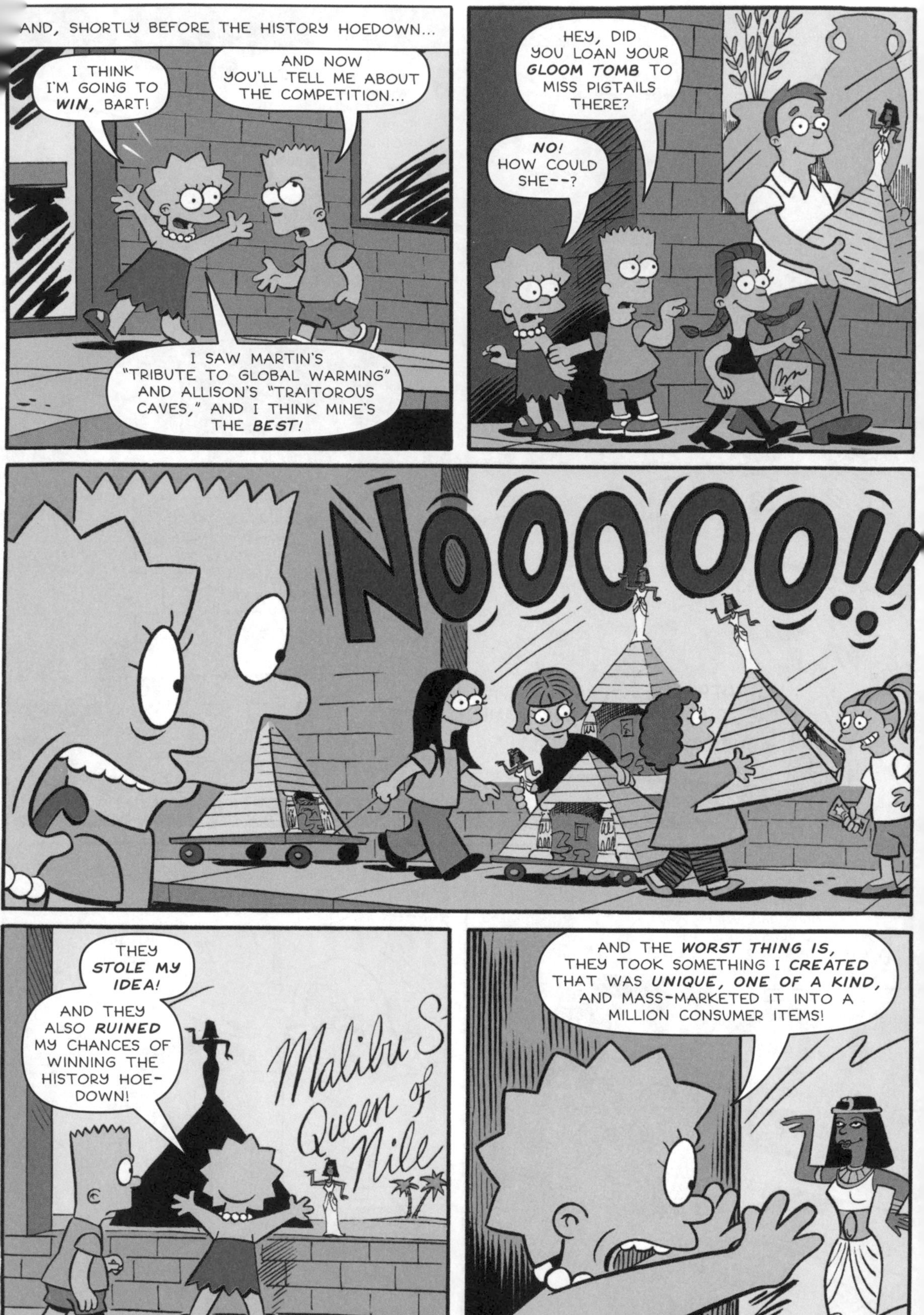

AND, SHORTLY BEFORE THE HISTORY HOEDOWN...
I THINK I'M GOING TO WIN, BART!
AND NOW YOU'LL TELL ME ABOUT THE COMPETITION...
I SAW MARTIN'S "TRIBUTE TO GLOBAL WARMING" AND ALLISON'S "TRAITOROUS CAVES," AND I THINK MINE'S THE BEST!
HEY, DID YOU LOAN YOUR GLOOM TOMB TO MISS PIGTAILS THERE?
NO! HOW COULD SHE--?
NOOOOO!!
THEY STOLE MY IDEA!
AND THEY ALSO RUINED MY CHANCES OF WINNING THE HISTORY HOE-DOWN!
Malibu S
Queen of Nile
AND THE WORST THING IS, THEY TOOK SOMETHING I CREATED THAT WAS UNIQUE, ONE OF A KIND, AND MASS-MARKETED IT INTO A MILLION CONSUMER ITEMS!

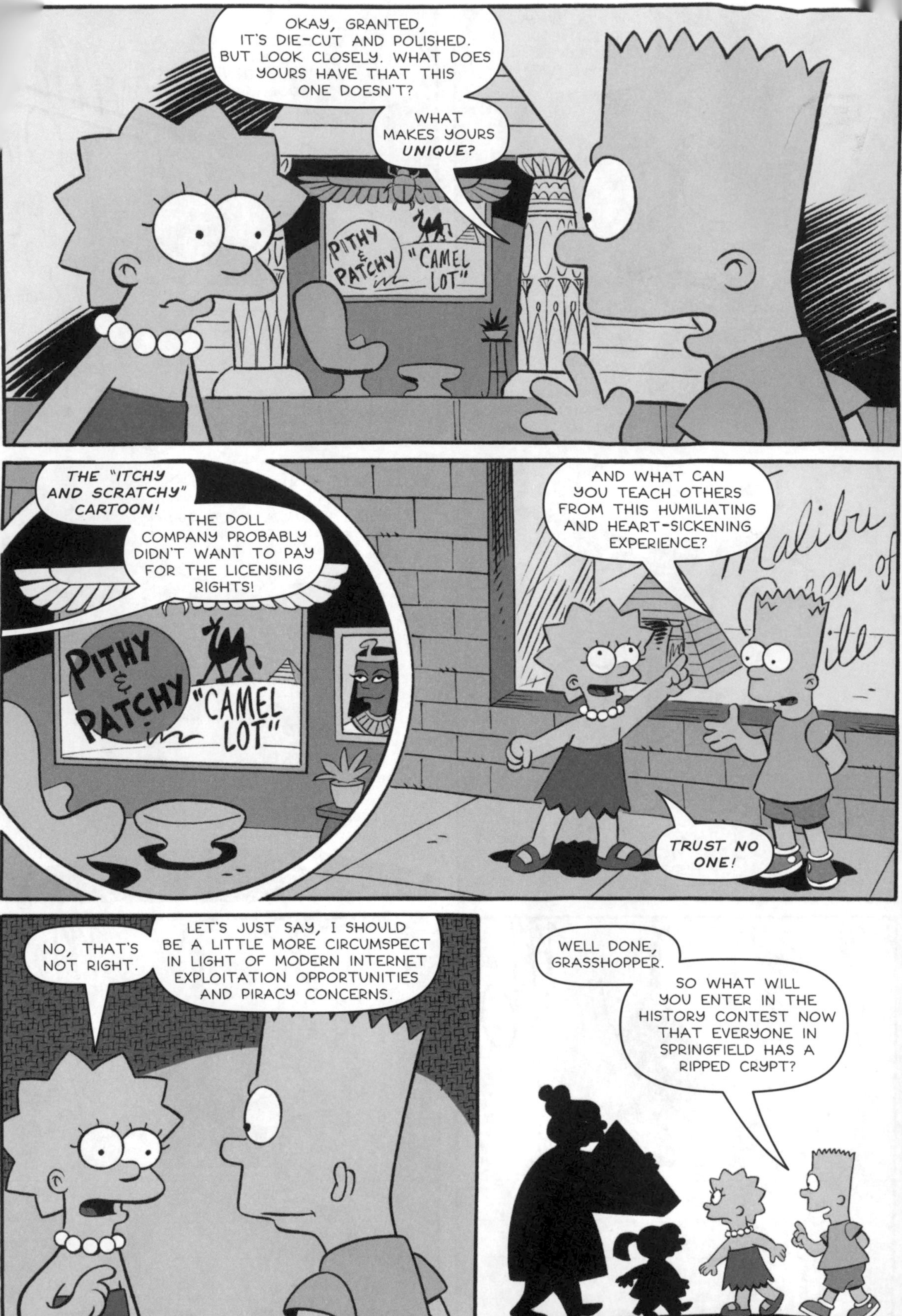
OKAY, GRANTED, IT'S DIE-CUT AND POLISHED. BUT LOOK CLOSELY. WHAT DOES YOURS HAVE THAT THIS ONE DOESN'T?
WHAT MAKES YOURS *UNIQUE?*
PITHY & PATCHY "CAMEL LOT"
THE "ITCHY AND SCRATCHY" CARTOON!
THE DOLL COMPANY PROBABLY DIDN'T WANT TO PAY FOR THE LICENSING RIGHTS!
PITHY & PATCHY "CAMEL LOT"
AND WHAT CAN YOU TEACH OTHERS FROM THIS HUMILIATING AND HEART-SICKENING EXPERIENCE?
TRUST NO ONE!
NO, THAT'S NOT RIGHT.
LET'S JUST SAY, I SHOULD BE A LITTLE MORE CIRCUMSPECT IN LIGHT OF MODERN INTERNET EXPLOITATION OPPORTUNITIES AND PIRACY CONCERNS.
WELL DONE, GRASSHOPPER.
SO WHAT WILL YOU ENTER IN THE HISTORY CONTEST NOW THAT EVERYONE IN SPRINGFIELD HAS A RIPPED CRYPT?

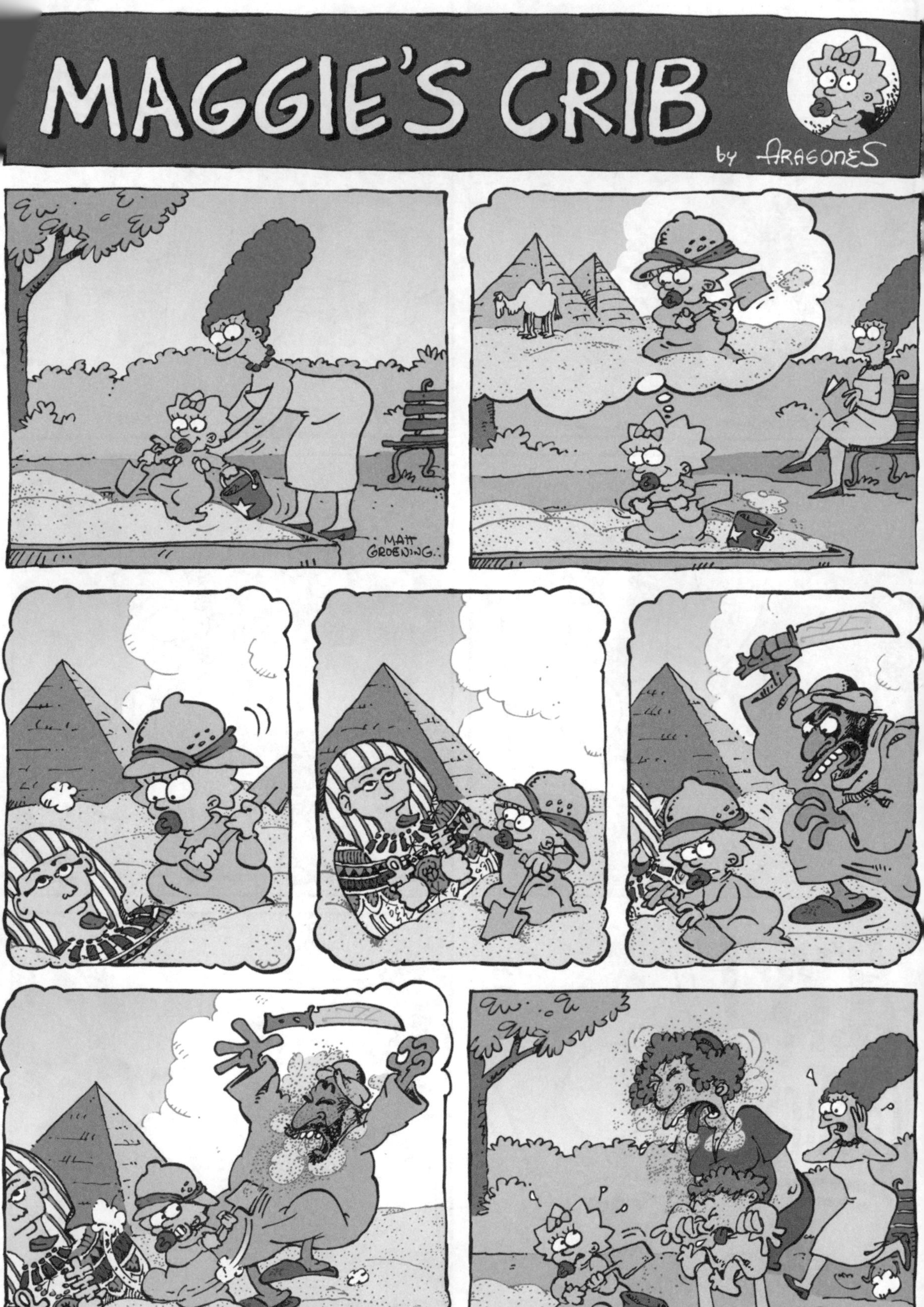
MAGGIE'S CRIB
by ARAGONES
MATT GROENING

SERGIO ARAGONÉS STORY & ART

ART VILLANUEVA COLORS

BILL MORRISON EDITOR

ROD & TODD PRAY-OFF

TONY DIGEROLAMO
SCRIPT

PHIL ORTIZ
PENCILS

MIKE ROTE
INKS

NATHAN HAMILL
COLORS

KAREN BATES
LETTERS

BILL MORRISON
EDITOR

THE END

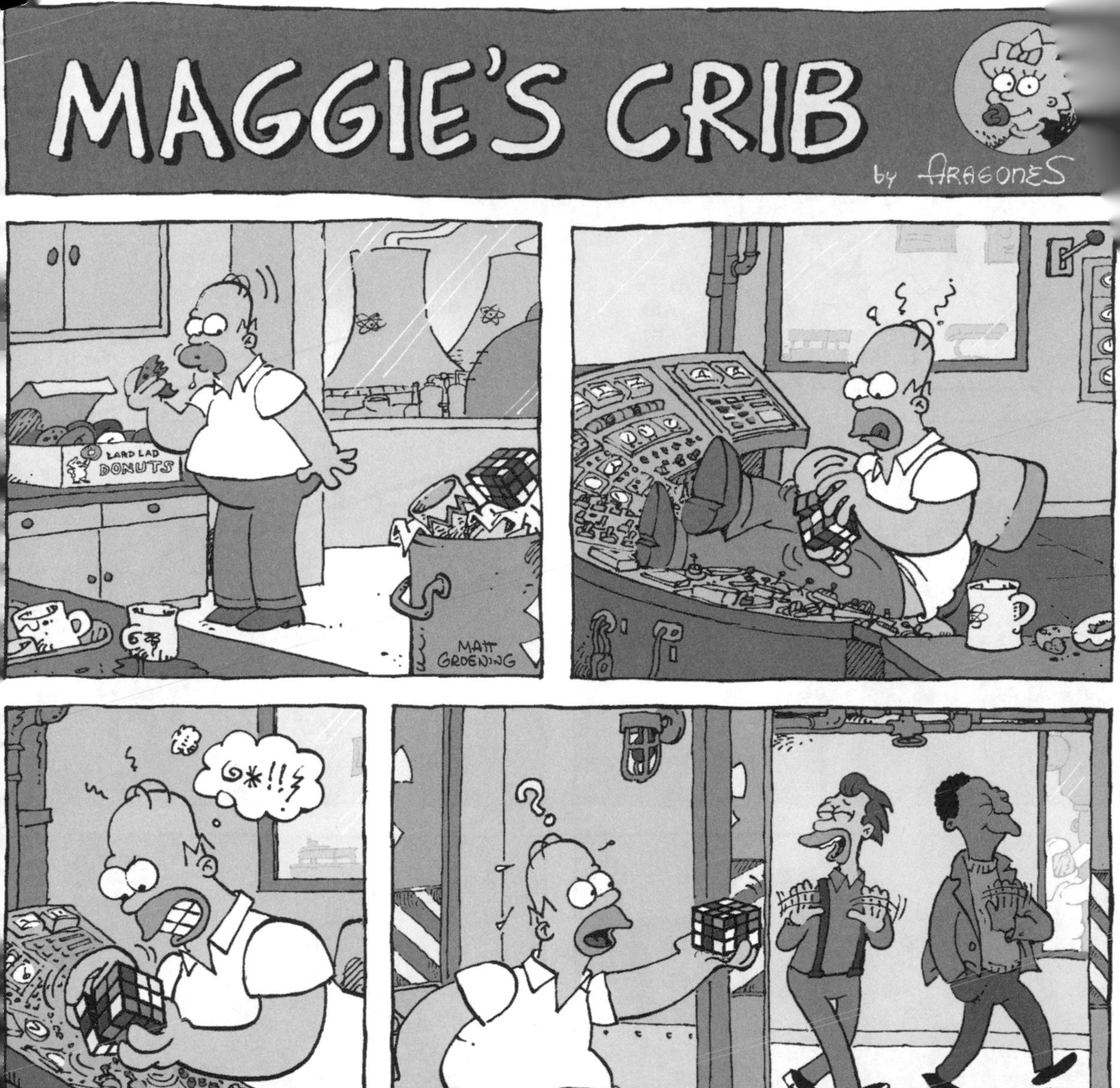
MAGGIE'S CRIB
by ARAGONES
LARD LAD DONUTS
MATT GROENING

SERGIO ARAGONÉS STORY & ART

ART VILLANUEVA COLORS

BILL MORRISON EDITOR

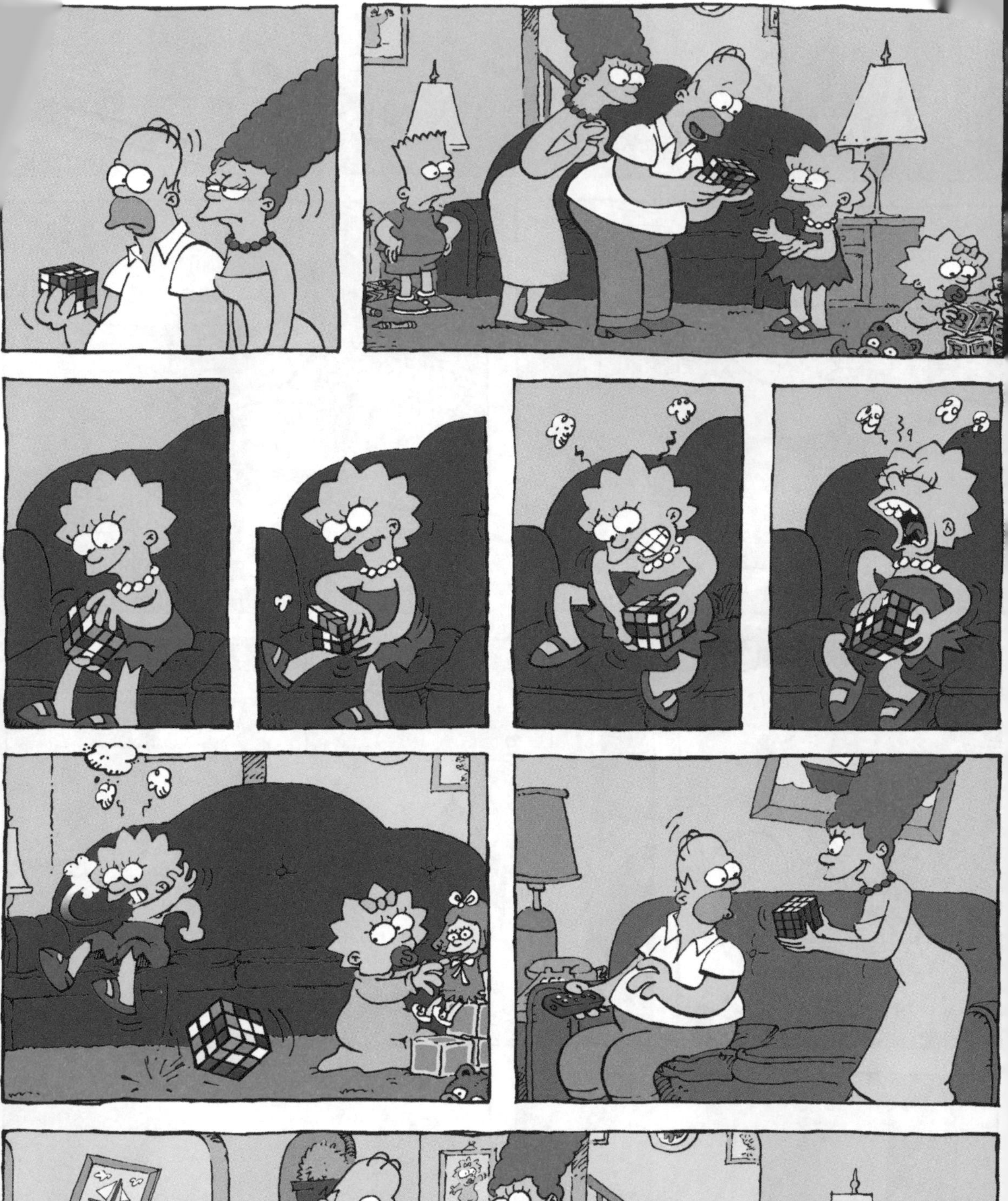

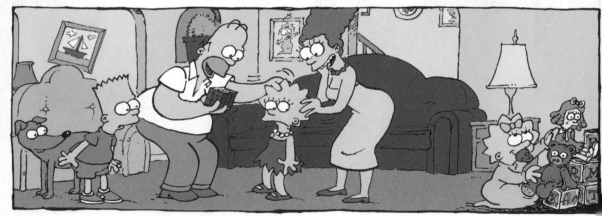

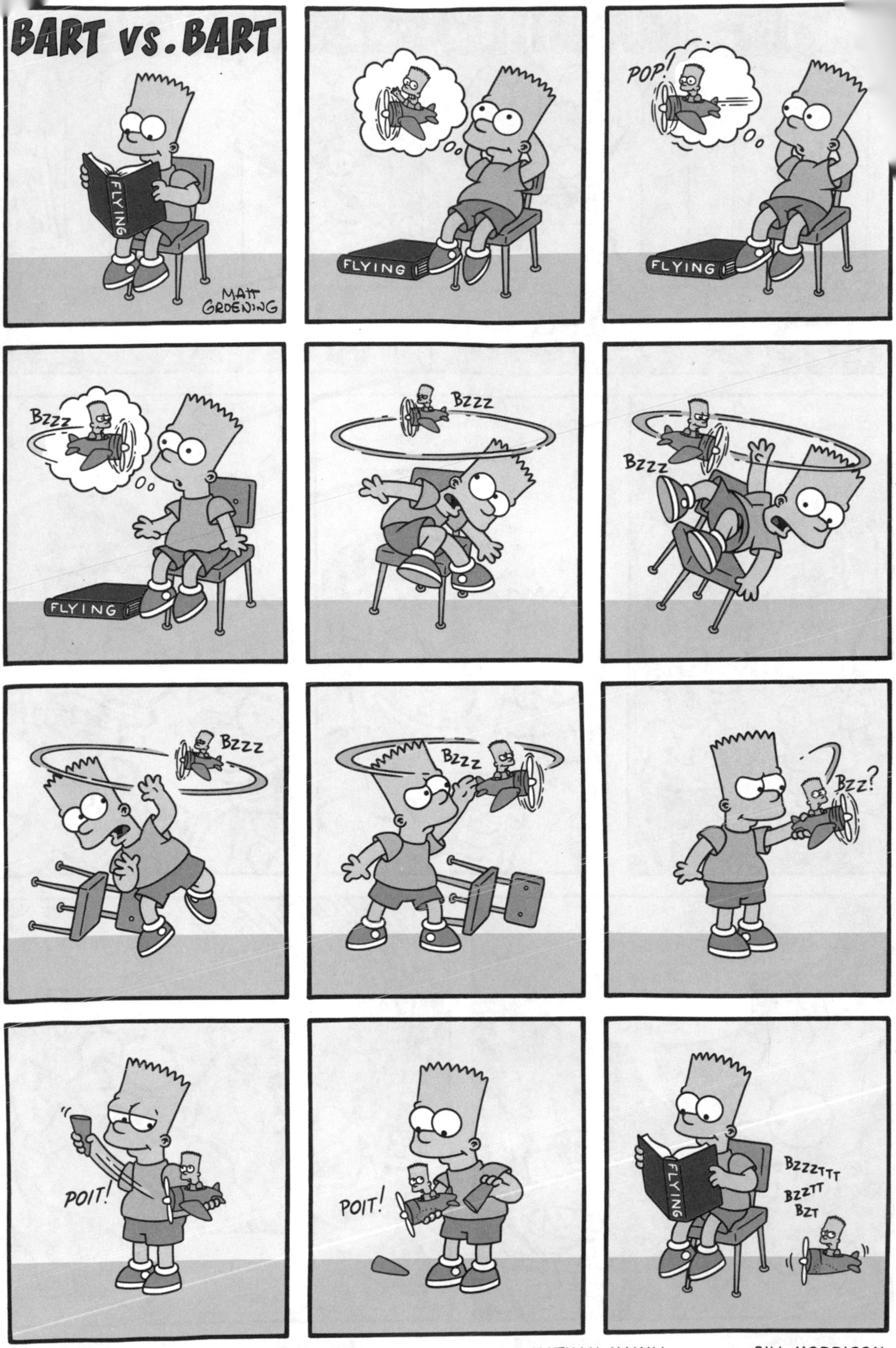
BART VS. BART
MATT GROENING
FLYING
FLYING
POP!
FLYING
BZZZ
FLYING
BZZZ
BZZZ
BZZZ
BZZZ
BZZ?
POIT!
POIT!
FLYING
BZZZTTT
BZZTT
BZT

MARY TRAINOR
STORY

MIKE ROTE
PENCILS & INKS

NATHAN HAMILL
COLORS

BILL MORRISON
EDITOR

EVAN DORKIN
STORY & ART

SARAH DYER
COLORS

KAREN BATES
LETTERS

BILL MORRISON
EDITOR

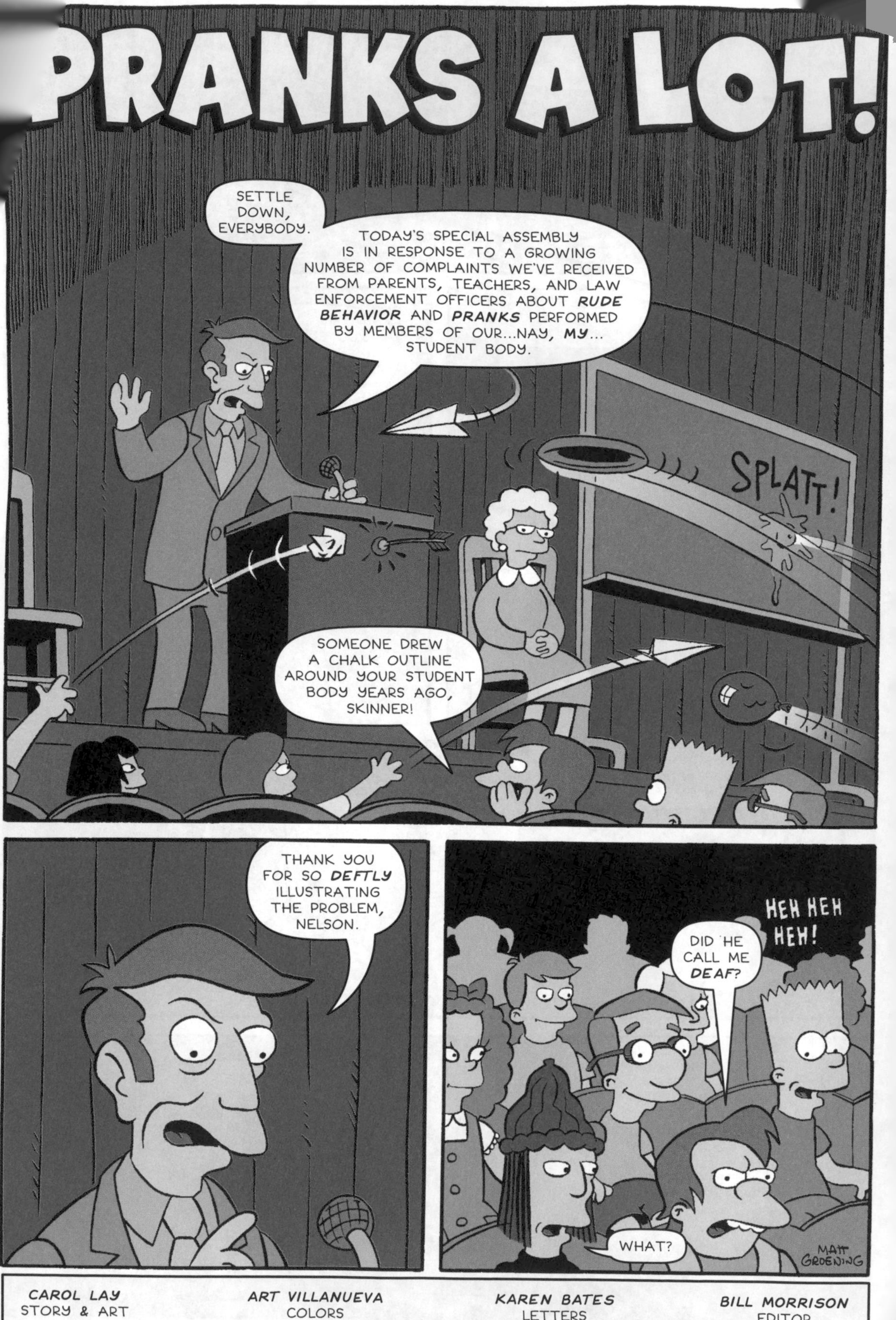
PRANKS A LOT!
SETTLE DOWN, EVERYBODY.
TODAY'S SPECIAL ASSEMBLY IS IN RESPONSE TO A GROWING NUMBER OF COMPLAINTS WE'VE RECEIVED FROM PARENTS, TEACHERS, AND LAW ENFORCEMENT OFFICERS ABOUT RUDE BEHAVIOR AND PRANKS PERFORMED BY MEMBERS OF OUR...NAY, MY... STUDENT BODY.
SPLATT!
SOMEONE DREW A CHALK OUTLINE AROUND YOUR STUDENT BODY YEARS AGO, SKINNER!
THANK YOU FOR SO DEFTLY ILLUSTRATING THE PROBLEM, NELSON.
HEH HEH HEH!
DID HE CALL ME DEAF?
WHAT?
MATT GROENING

CAROL LAY STORY & ART | ***ART VILLANUEVA*** COLORS | ***KAREN BATES*** LETTERS | ***BILL MORRISON*** EDITOR

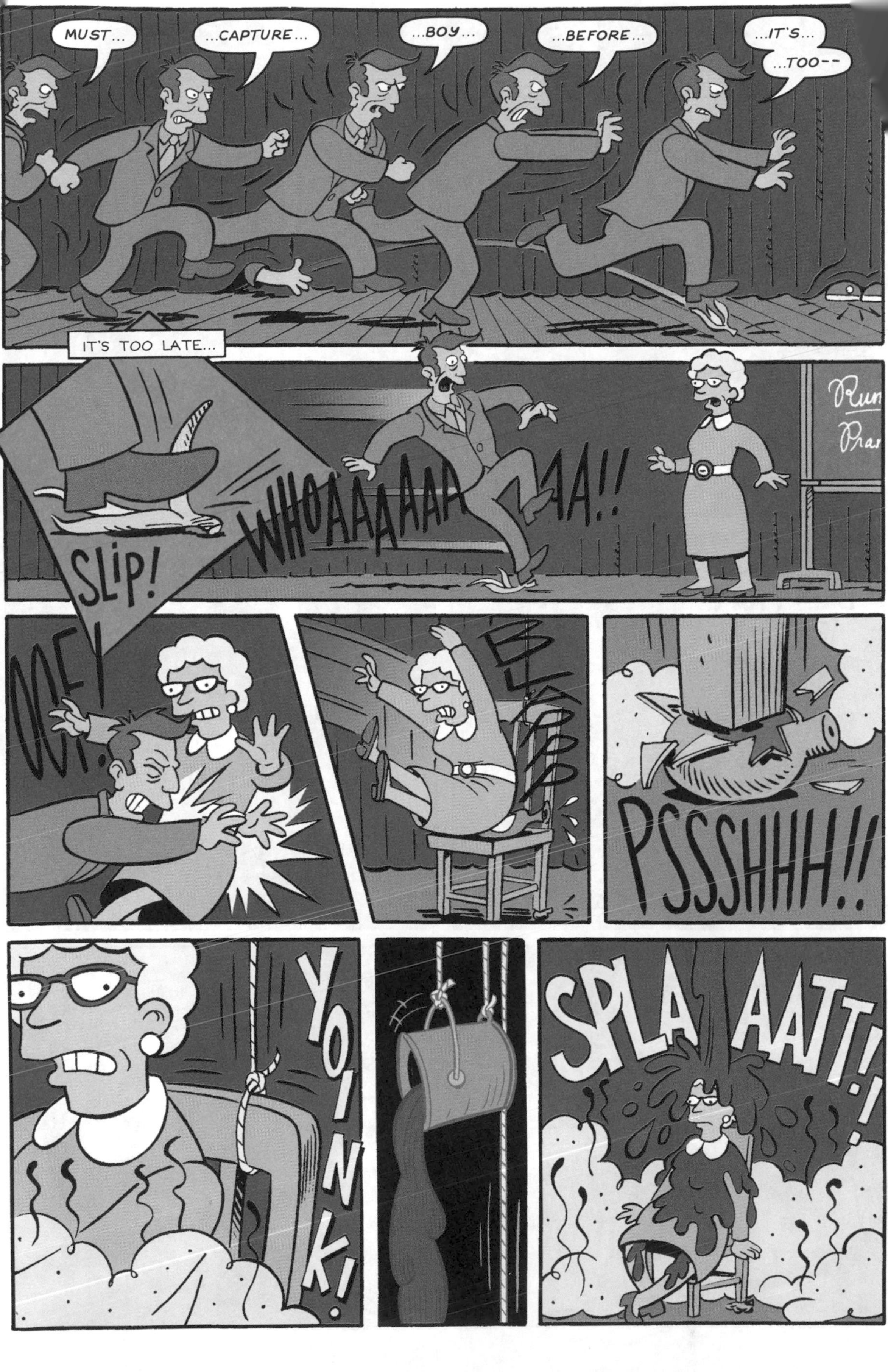
MUST...
...CAPTURE...
...BOY...
...BEFORE...
...IT'S...
...TOO--
IT'S TOO LATE...
SLIP!
WHOAAAAAA
AA!!
OOF!
PSSSHHH!!
YOINK!
SPLA
AATT!!

BY AND BY...

AND THE WINNER IS...

BART SIMPSON FOR "WHAT'S THAT SMELL?"

OH, *MAN*, THIS IS THE *BEST MOMENT* OF MY *ENTIRE LIFE!*

BEFORE WE PRESENT THE AWARD, PLEASE BE SEATED FOR A SPECIAL TREAT, COURTESY OF YOUR TWO ESCORTS.

NO PROBLEMO! LAY IT ON ME!

WHA--?! *HEY! I CAN'T MOVE!* MY CLOTHES ARE *GLUED* TO THE *SEAT!*

HUH?!

ROARRRRRR!!

WHOAAAAA!!

HEY! WHAT'S THE BIG IDEA?!

LEMME DOWN!

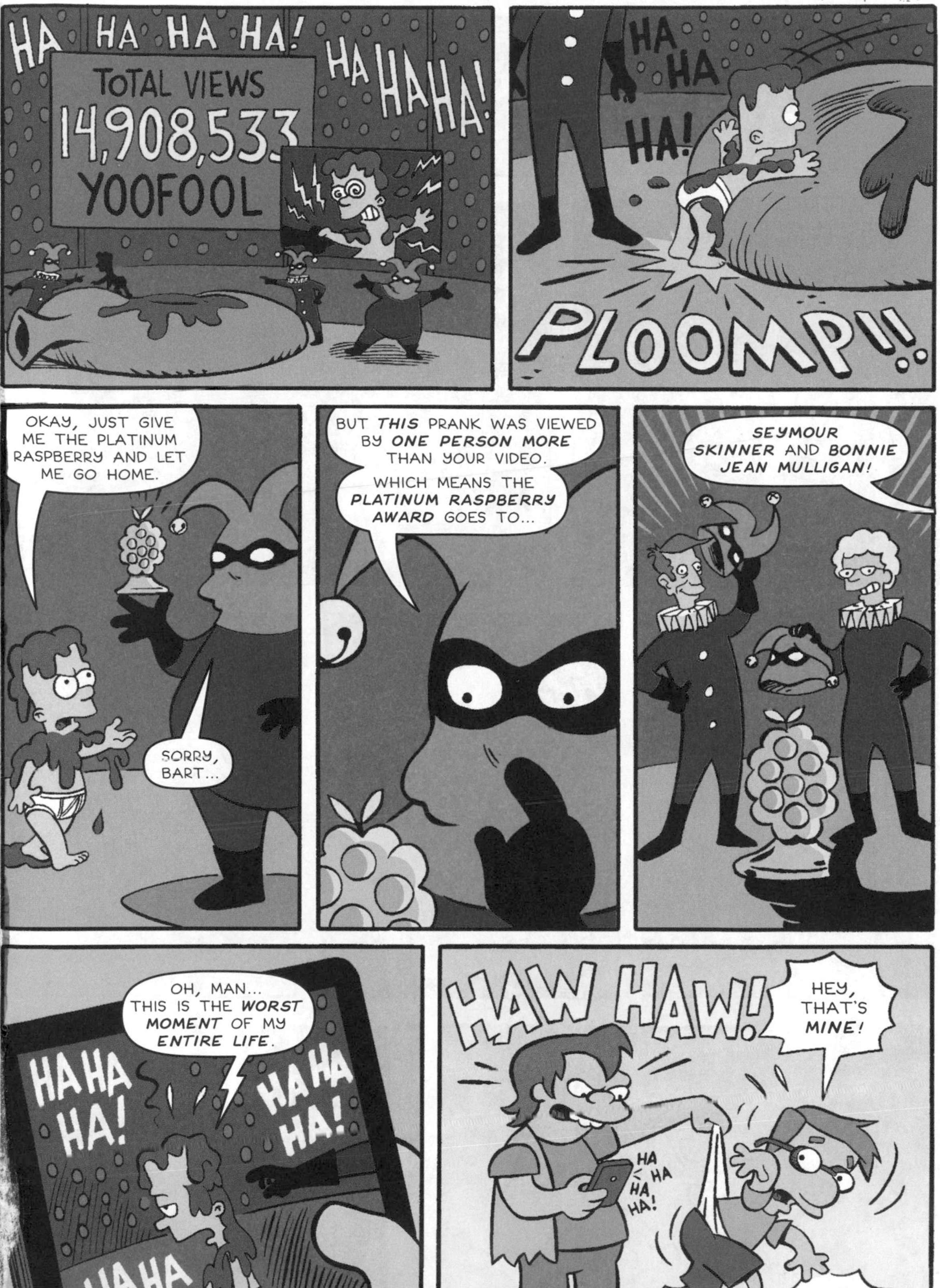
HA HA HA HA!
TOTAL VIEWS
14,908,533
YOOFOOL
HA HAHA!
HA HA HA!
PLOOMP!!
OKAY, JUST GIVE ME THE PLATINUM RASPBERRY AND LET ME GO HOME.
SORRY, BART...
BUT THIS PRANK WAS VIEWED BY ONE PERSON MORE THAN YOUR VIDEO.
WHICH MEANS THE PLATINUM RASPBERRY AWARD GOES TO...
SEYMOUR SKINNER AND BONNIE JEAN MULLIGAN!
OH, MAN... THIS IS THE WORST MOMENT OF MY ENTIRE LIFE.
HA HA HA!
HA HA HA!
HA HA HA!
HAW HAW!
HEY, THAT'S MINE!
HA HA HA HA!
GIVE IT BACK!
THE END

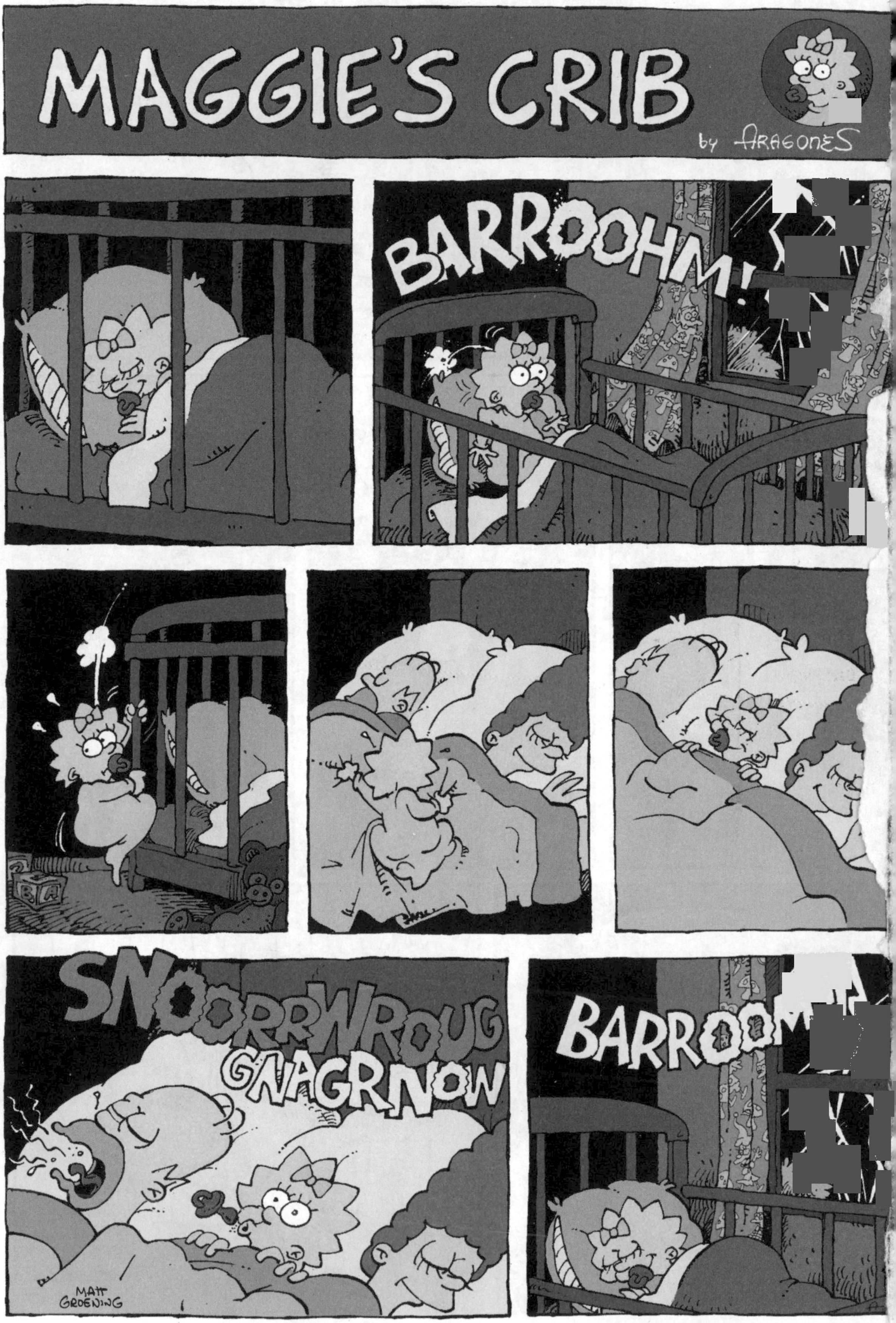
MAGGIE'S CRIB
by ARAGONES
BARROOHM!
SNOORRRWROUG
GNAGRNOW
BARROO
MATT GROENING

SERGIO ARAGONÉS STORY & ART | **ART VILLANUEVA** COLORS | **BILL MORRISON** EDITOR